The National Trust Book of
Fruit and Vegetable Cookery

COOKERY BOOKS PUBLISHED BY
THE NATIONAL TRUST

The Book of National Trust Recipes

The National Trust Book of Fish Cookery

The National Trust Book of Healthy Eating

The National Trust Book of Tea-Time Recipes

THE NATIONAL TRUST
BOOK OF
FRUIT AND VEGETABLE
COOKERY

Simone Sekers

THE NATIONAL TRUST

First published in Great Britain in 1991 by
National Trust Enterprises Limited
36 Queen Anne's Gate
London SW1H 9AS

British Library Cataloguing in Publication Data

Sekers, Simone
 The National Trust book of fruit and vegetable
 cookery.
 1. Vegetables. Fruit. Cookery
 I. Title II. National Trust
 641.64

ISBN 0-7078-0131-1

Illustrations by Elizabeth Jane Lloyd

Designed by Gail Engert

Phototypeset in Monotype Lasercomp Bembo 270
by Southern Positives and Negatives (SPAN),
Lingfield, Surrey

Printed in England by
Butler & Tanner Ltd, Frome, Somerset

CONTENTS

ACKNOWLEDGEMENTS

My thanks go to all those who helped with information for this book, in particular:

Stephen Biggins, Pat Brittain, David Brown, Colin Brunt, Ted Bullock, David Crosbie, Susan Denyer, Hugh Dixon, Graham Donachie, Stephen Emmerson, Barry Futter, Julian Gibbs, Diane Henry, Ian Hughes, Isabelle King, Jenny Kirk, Stuart Knight, John Maddison, Christine Milsom, Terry Mulqueen, Diana Owen, Alan Paston-Williams, J. Pine, Maria Ramsay, Sue Renshaw, Lou Richardson, Christopher Rowell, Chris Smith, Richard Squires, R. Taylor, John Teven, Paul Underwood, Catherine Usher, Michael Walker, Margaret Willes, Samantha Wyndham.

Permission to use passages from *Uppark and its People*, by Margaret Meade-Fetherstonhaugh and Oliver Warner, has been kindly granted by the publishers, Unwin Hyman Ltd.

For David, supportive husband and gardener,
and for all the gardeners in the National Trust
whose enthusiasm and dedication
give endless inspiration and pleasure.

CONVERSIONS

The following approximate conversions are used in this book.

$\frac{1}{2}$ oz	12 g	1 teaspoon	5 ml	
1 oz	25 g	1 dessertspoon	10 ml	
2 oz	50 g	1 tablespoon	15 ml	
3 oz	75 g	1 fluid oz	30 ml	
4 oz	125 g	4 fluid oz	100 ml	
5 oz	150 g	5 fluid oz	125 ml	
6 oz	175 g	8 fluid oz	225 ml	
7 oz	200 g	10 fluid oz	300 ml	
8 oz	225 g	12 fluid oz	360 ml	
12 oz	350 g	15 fluid oz	450 ml	
1 lb	450 g			
$1\frac{1}{2}$ lb	675 g	$\frac{1}{4}$ pint	150 ml	
2 lb	900 g	$\frac{1}{2}$ pint	250 ml	
		1 pint	500 ml	
$\frac{1}{4}$ in	6 mm	$1\frac{1}{2}$ pints	750 ml	
$\frac{1}{2}$ in	1.25 cm	$1\frac{3}{4}$ pints	1 litre	
$\frac{3}{4}$ in	2 cm	2 pints	1.25 litres	
1 in	2.5 cm			
$1\frac{1}{2}$ in	4 cm	Gas Mark		
2 in	5 cm	1	275°F	140°C
6 in	15 cm	2	300°F	150°C
7 in	18 cm	3	325°F	160°C
8 in	20 cm	4	350°F	180°C
9 in	23 cm	5	375°F	190°C
10 in	25 cm	6	400°F	200°C
12 in	30.5 cm	7	425°F	220°C
		8	450°F	230°C

AMERICAN EQUIVALENTS

As the following conversions are approximate, it is essential to use all American, or all metric, or all imperial measures when following the recipes.

Dried orange flowers Dried lavender flowers	1 US cup	=	1oz	=	25g
Crushed biscuits Dried breadcrumbs	1 US cup	=	2oz	=	50g
Peas Flaked almonds	1 US cup	=	4oz	=	125g
Flour Cornflour Dried fruit	1 US cup	=	5oz	=	150g
Fresh fruit Chopped peel	1 US cup	=	6oz	=	175g
Sugar Pearl barley	1 US cup	=	7oz	=	200g
Fats Cream cheese	1 US cup	=	8oz	=	225g
Apple purée Fruit pulp	1 US cup	=	9oz	=	250g
Liquids	1 US cup	=	8fl oz	=	225ml
	1 US cup	=	16fl oz	=	475ml

Introduction

INTRODUCTION

EGETABLE gardens took many centuries to evolve from the herb beds which produced the 'worts', 'scallions' and 'roots' that formed the vegetable matter of a medieval diet to the cornucopia of fruit, vegetables and herbs which were to be found within the walls of an Edwardian kitchen garden.

The National Trust reflects these centuries in the many styles of its gardens, from the tranquility of herb gardens such as those at Acorn Bank in Cumbria, and at Buckland Abbey in Devon, to the horticultural 'bustle' of the vegetable garden at Quarry Bank Mill in Cheshire, and the charming walled garden at Felbrigg in Norfolk. What has not yet emerged, although it is being planned by the Trust, is the ultimate kitchen garden, with its rows of perfectly kept glass and hot-houses full of exotic fruits – melons, grapes, nectarines, even pineapples – its cages of soft fruit, its serried ranks of perfectly spaced onions, carrots and lettuces and its wall-trained apricots and plums.

Such a garden presents a daunting task; the ratio of labour to plant is high and very expensive. No wonder huge 4-acre plots such as that at Calke Abbey in Derbyshire fell into disuse. This remains the paddock it became after the Second World War, the splendid walls enclosing rough grass and the whole area presided over by a ruin of an orangery in which a stubborn palm tree seems determined to last until better days return. And they are coming. Funds are being raised to restore the orangery, and if the kitchen garden is still a paddock, the next door Physic Garden, a mere $1\frac{1}{2}$ acres, is now a thriving mixture of vegetables, soft fruit and orchard trees, with glass houses and cucumber frames once again being put to good use.

Kitchen gardens such as those at Barrington Court in Somerset, Upton House in Warwickshire, and West Green House in Hampshire, have been maintained by the families who continue to live as tenants of the Trust in such houses, rather than by the Trust itself – a practical solution which can work very well. The Trust, sensibly, has put its considerable expertise to work in a less labour-intensive area, that of growing fruit trees whether as wall-fruit, as at Westbury Court Garden in Gloucestershire and Felbrigg, or as orchards like those at Berrington Hall in Herefordshire. At Berrington, a mutually beneficial arrangement between the Trust and the National Council for the Conservation of Plants and Gardens has resulted in a splendid collection of more than fifty varieties of apple, almost half of them indigenous to Hereford-shire, a famous apple-growing area. At Erddig in north Wales, wall-trained apples and pears form a sumptuous display of autumn fruit and a frame for an orchard of trees planted in a quincunx design; more modestly, the orchard at Trerice, the quiet grey manor house buried in a valley near Newquay in Cornwall, contains local varieties of fruit, as does the orchard at Nunnington Hall in North Yorkshire.

All these gardens are noted and well-visited. What I enjoyed while researching this book was discovering those which were not mentioned anywhere. The Trust is often unduly modest about its gardens, but it does give visitors a chance to discover for themselves a gate in a wall which reveals a haven of peace and warmth, of old stone honeycombed by the nails, long since rusted away, that provided the framework for trees which have now broken their bounds and grow with greater freedom but with less productivity.

One of the Trust's well-kept secret gardens is at Fenton House, hidden in a labyrinth of narrow streets in the heart of London's Hampstead. Within the walled garden of this late seventeenth-century house, reached by descending the steps from the main formal garden, stands a small orchard undersown with a mixture of wild flowers. Beyond lies the kitchen garden, planted with an informal mixture of vegetables, herbs and flowers all crammed into this sheltered space. John Teven, the gardener, makes no claim that this is a 'period' garden. An old variety of cos lettuce grows cheek by jowl with 'new' Chinese leaf vegetables, and both Victorian glass cloches and twentieth-century rabbit netting protect vulnerable young plants. Mr Teven is amused by London children comparing the garden to a supermarket – they had never before seen onions and apples actually growing. A particularly charming view of the garden is to be had from one of the attic rooms of the house, where, seen from above, the neat rows of vegetables contrast beautifully with the sprawling nasturtiums and bright blue chicory flowers of late summer when I visited. Most kitchen gardens were planted well away and out of sight so such a pleasing view is not often possible, but the cramped conditions of a London garden mean it is possible to appreciate, from within the house, the progression of vegetables through the seasons.

In this sort of garden it is equally easy to imagine the progression of its produce to the kitchen, and then on to the dining-room table. The changing fashions of horticulture have always been mirrored by cookery books. By the end of the seventeenth-century, for instance, salads were as popular as they are today and merited a whole book to themselves, John Evelyn's celebrated *Acetaria*, in which he lists at least three dozen suitable plants; however, he does suggest pickling the 'small green fruit' which sometimes appear on potato plants, unaware of their poisonous solanine content. In the middle of the next century the 'gourmandine' pea makes an appearance in another cookery book, almost certainly the mange-tout pea which has only recently made a reappearance on our tables. Potatoes slowly gain space, both in books and in gardens, first cooked as a sweet dish, as were most root vegetables (see Hannah Glasse's recipe on p.33) and finally in the most frugal of dishes, Vegetable Pie, on p.44.

By the eighteenth century, all sorts of fruits and vegetables were flourishing, not only in the gardens of the very rich, but in modest yeomen's houses, too. There were writers who were interested in both botany and gastronomy, like Richard Bradley, a Fellow of the Royal Society, who gave the first recipe for pineapple ever to appear in an English cookery book; the first pineapple ever grown in England had already appeared, grown by one John Rose and presented to Charles II. A version of the painting describing this memorable event hangs at Ham House in Surrey. In 1747, Hannah Glasse published her delightful book *The Art of Cookery made Plain and Easy*, which is full of recipes that give vegetables their full worth. Recipes such as 'A Ragoo of Beans with a Force' you will find on p.36 of this book, a delicious combination of French beans in a light sauce served with a carrot soufflé. These recipes are in accord with light and elegant Georgian architecture, furniture, paintings and even literature. Gradually, as Queen Victoria's reign lengthened, food became darker, heavier and more elaborate.

By the end of the nineteenth century, vegetable recipes were just beginning to show signs of how they were to become abused by bad cooks. Mrs Beeton gives many instructions for lengthy boilings in plenty of water with a good pinch of soda, a tradition which was to last long, far too long, into this century. Fruit still held pride of place, especially in Victorian and Edwardian households where elaborate desserts and displays of hot-house fruits were a necessary part of large dinner parties and matters of pride to cook and gardener alike, while wholesome apple pies and stewed gooseberries were considered sensible nursery food.

While the Trust's tea-rooms and restaurants offer many excellent dishes (and I have included several, such as Bitter Orange Tea Bread on p.94, and Apple and Elderberry Tart on p.51), I wanted those which specifically conjured up the everyday life of the house and its garden. So it is from old, English cookery books that I have taken the recipes for this book, books contemporary with the time the house, or that particular part of the garden, were at their most flourishing and animated. Thus the recipes which came to mind when visiting Calke were from early Victorian books, such as Eliza Acton's *Modern Cookery*, published at a time when Sir George Crewe was leading a social life, entertaining local worthies. After his death, Calke drew down its shutters again and the family returned to their reclusive quiet, but before that the cooking practised in those cavernous, echoing kitchens would have been economical but good, drawing on the produce of that immense walled kitchen garden. The book which epitomises the revival of interest in simple, clean flavours between the world wars – and thus the herb garden at Sissinghurst in Kent, or the arched pear trees of Bateman's in East Sussex – is Mrs Leyel's *The Gentle Art of Cookery*. For the wholesome nutrition that ties in with the Apprentice House garden at Styal, I turned to the finger-wagging chapters on how to feed the poor from Victorian manuals of housekeeping.

Sometimes it is necessary to use a little gastronomic licence, where the garden does not always reflect the exact date of the house, or where such a garden no longer exists. Nevertheless, it is possible to imagine what dishes were eaten in those rooms, and to imagine the gardener bringing in their components from whatever garden existed when the house was enjoying its heyday. What I want to share is the spirit of place which is as strongly emphasised when you stand in an orchard, or crush the aromatic leaves of some herb, or marvel at the elegance of an orangery heavy with the scent of orange blossom, as by any carefully preserved artefact.

The Herb Garden

THE HERB GARDEN

T COULD be said that herb gardens were the first kitchen gardens, for the small range of root crops and brassicas that constituted most of the vegetables eaten up until the seventeenth century was included under that heading. That one oversimplified word has come to mean only the few plants which we use nowadays for flavouring – the mints, thymes, sages and marjorams, rosemary, parsley, chervil and tarragon. In fact, although the botanical definition given in Chambers Dictionary describes them as plants with no woody stem above ground, the best general definition is that they are *useful* plants, whether in the kitchen, house or medicine chest.

At Acorn Bank, there has long been a tradition of cultivating medicinal herbs, since it was used by the Knights Templar who had a religious house on this site in the thirteenth century which was later tranferred to the Knights of the Hospital of St John. Within these old brick walls the National Trust grows a collection of 250, mainly medicinal, plants, some of which contain potent poisons in unexpected forms, despite their benign appearance. Lily of the valley and wood anemones, both innocent-looking spring flowers, are both poisonous. So too are foxgloves, deadly nightshade (hence the name, although Victorian beauties used belladonna drops to dilate the pupils of their eyes and make them look large and lustrous), laburnum, cuckoo pint, cherry laurel and green hellebore; all lurk here, valuable for their medicinal properties, but poisonous when used without care and the right knowledge.

The long borders at Acorn Bank hold many interesting and unusual plants which demonstrate the wide spectrum of the uses of herbs: Dyers' Greenweed, for instance, has flowering tops which are used to produce a yellow dye, but which is also a remedy for dropsy and rheumatism; or Indian Physic, which is used by American Indians as an emetic and for dyspepsia and constipation. It was here, too, that I learnt that the familiar seed-pods of Honesty, shaped like the full moon, were thought to cure lunacy – a neat association of ideas if not entirely effective.

The following tips are for some safe herbal remedies:

An infusion of foxglove leaves added to a vase is one way of prolonging the life of cut flowers.

To ease toothache, especially after the tooth has been extracted, heat dried camomile flowers in the oven and fold them into a clean, soft handkerchief. Hold this pad against the face until it cools, and repeat as often as necessary.

Camomile is a pleasant way of achieving a good night's sleep. Put a generous pinch of the flowers into a small teapot and pour boiling water over; infuse for 5 minutes and drink as hot as possible, sweetened with a spoonful of honey since it is bitter.

Comfrey was also known as 'knitbone' for its ability to heal. Culpeper describes the roots as 'so powerful to consolidate and knit together, that if they be boiled with disseevered pieces of flesh in a pot, it will join them together again'; while I have not experimented to that ghoulish extent, I have used a poultice of the leaves, applied hot, to a sprained ankle with very good effect.

Sage is also good for easing sprains, and an old recipe suggests infusing a handful of the leaves in $\frac{1}{4}$ pint of hot vinegar for 15 minutes, before applying this poultice as hot as possible to the sprain.

Sage was much used to cure gum troubles, too, and it certainly makes a pleasant mouthwash. Use a cold infusion night and morning, especially if the gums are swollen or sore.

Borage has won a place in the hearts of all those who enjoy drinking Pimms in the summer, since it forms part of the approved garnish to each glass. The origins of adding this herb to wine or wine cups go back a very long way. John Evelyn, in *Acetaria*, his discourse on herbs and salads published in 1699, suggested adding sprigs to wine 'to revive the Hypochondriac and chear the hard Student'.

An elaborate herbal preventive, rather than remedy, is that of Hannah Glasse. Her 'Receipt against the Plague' is included in *The Art of Cookery*, and was, if nothing else, a pleasant smell and welcomed on that score when plague was rife. Fortunately we have no way of testing it these days, but it might work in a flu' epidemic:

A Receipt against the Plague

Take of Rue, Sage, Mint, Rosemary, Wormwood and Lavender, a Handful of each, infuse them together in a Gallon of White Wine-Vinegar, put the whole into a Stone-pot closely covered up, upon warm Wood Ashes for four Days: After which draw off (or strain through fine Flannel) the Liquid, and put it into Bottles well corked; and into every Quart Bottle, put a Quarter of an Ounce of Camphire. With this Preparation, wash your Mouth, and rub your Loins and your Temples every Day; snuff a little up your Nostrils when you go into the Air, and carry about you a Bit of Spunge dipped in the same, in order to smell to upon all Occasions, especially when you are near any Place or Person that is infected. They write, that four Malefactors (who had robbed the infested Houses, and murdered the People during the Course of the Plague) owned, when they came to the Gallows, that they had preserved themselves from the Contagion, by using the above Medicine only; and that they went the whole time from House to House, without any fear of the Distemper.

The herbals of the fifteenth and sixteenth centuries were invaluable to those who could read and so make use of the wisdom they contained. John Gerard, whose massive *Herbal, or Generall Historie of Plantes* was first published in 1597, pays tribute to 'Master Lyte, a Worshipfull Gentleman' for his translation of Dodoen's *Niewe Herball* from 'French into English' – in fact it was from the Flemish, and became so popular that it was known as Lyte's Herbal and was reprinted many times. Henry Lyte lived at Lytes Cary, near Ilchester in Somerset, home to the Lyte family for 500 years and now owned by the National Trust.

Such herbals make interesting and absorbing reading today; I found, for instance, when I moved to a garden with quick-draining sandy soil, that cow manure would be more suitable as a fertiliser than horse dung. I came across this useful bit of information while reading John Parkinson's introduction to his chapter on kitchen gardens, in his Herbal of 1633:

The stable soyle of horses is best and more proper for any colde grounds, for being the hottest, it will cause any the seedes for this Garden to prosper well, and be more forward then in any other ground that is not so holpen [helped]. The stable soyle of Cattell is of a colder and moister nature, and is

therefore more proper for the hot sandy or gravelly grounds,
and although it bee longer before it bee brought to mould
then that of horse, yet it will outlast it more then twice
so long.

Sound advice, more than 350 years old.

The picture most of us have of a herb garden is one of gently
fragrant flavouring plants, lavender especially, old roses whose
petals are particularly suitable for making pot-pourri, the soft
colours and grey leaves of rosemary, sage, thyme and rue,
punctuated by the deeper evergreen bay and myrtle. This sort
of romantic, rather than practical, herb garden is what Vita
Sackville-West had in mind for Sissinghurst, although she wrote,
ruefully, in one of her gardening articles for the *Observer* that
'my own small herb-garden is always encouragingly popular –
with the sentimentalists whom I know fatally in advance are going
to say that it is full of old-world charm'.

Well, I too become a sentimentalist in this garden, now one of the
most popular of all those owned by the Trust, and planted at a
time when there was indeed a rather dewy-eyed rekindling of
affection for the architecture and gardening styles, even the
cookery, of the sixteenth and seventeenth centuries. The recipe
which follows, for pot-pourri, comes from a book that exactly
typifies this feeling. Published in 1927 and called, winsomely,
A Book of Scents and Dishes, its author, Dorothy Allhusen, gathered
together old family recipes from around the country. Several
come from Vita Sackville-West herself while she and her husband,
Harold Nicolson, were still living at Long Barn and before they
had moved to nearby Sissinghurst, but the ingredients listed must
have given her some idea of what to include in her herb garden:

POT-POURRI (1750)

Gather dry, Double Violets, Rose Leaves, Lavender, Myrtle
flowers, Verbena, Bay leaves, Rosemary, Balm, Musk,
Geranium. Pick these from the stalks and dry on paper in the
sun for a day or two before putting them in a jar. This should
be a large white one, well glazed, with a close-fitting cover,
also a piece of card the exact size of the jar, which you must
keep pressed down on the flowers. Keep a new wooden
spoon to stir the salt and flowers from the bottom, before you
put in a fresh layer of bay salt above and below every layer of
flowers. Have ready of spices, plenty of Cinnamon, Mace,
Nutmeg and Pepper and Lemon Peel pounded. For a large

jar ½lb Orris Root, 1oz Storax, 1oz Gum Benjamin, 2oz Calamino Aromatico (the powdered dried root of Sweet Sedge *Acorus calamus*), 2grs [grains] Musk and a small quantity of oil of Rhodium. The spice and gum to be added when you have collected all the flowers your intend to put in. Mix all well together, press it down well, and spread bay salt on the top to exclude the air until the January or February following. Keep the jar in a cool dry place.

This old recipe calls for ingredients which are hard to come by these days, and it is tempting simply to buy pot-pourri ready made, restoring its scent when necessary by adding one of the reviver oils available. But these can often have a heavy, synthetic smell, nothing like the ethereal fragrance that so entranced Humphry Repton when he stayed at Uppark in Sussex. In a letter to Sir Harry Fetherstonhaugh in October 1815, he wrote: 'and I may truly say that in no place have I ever seen such accurate attention to olfactory joy as at Uppark – every room has its depot of odours for permanent use'.

A Modern Pot-Pourri

To make a similar 'depot of odours', try combining the dried leaves of the following plants:

Lemon verbena (*Lippia citriodora*) – a tender plant best grown in pots which can be given shelter from winter frosts; Scented geranium; Rosemary; Bergamot; Mint – particularly the eau-de-Cologne and pineapple mints; Thyme; Artemisia; Myrtle; Sweetbriar; Bay.

To these you can add dried lavender flowers and dried rose petals, particularly from highly scented old varieties. Follow the instructions for the 1750 pot-pourri, adding plenty of fine sea salt between each layer, and spices, whole rather than powdered: crushed cinnamon sticks, cloves, coriander seeds and cardamom pods. Keep in a covered jar, removing the lid only when you want to scent the room. Keeping out the light as well as the air will help the scent to last until the next season's crop of scents is ready to harvest. Gentle pruning of old roses when harvesting their petals can often encourage a repeat flowering later in the season.

Scented geraniums can come in various guises, some with variegated leaves smelling of lemons, some with delicate grey leaves smelling of camphor. The rose-scented geranium gives its scent and flavour with great benefit to *compôtes* of blackcurrants, or blackberries, or to damsons. A leaf placed at the bottom of the tin when baking a sponge-cake can flavour it sufficiently to make it into something very special when served with a filling of strawberries or raspberries and cream. To decorate such a cake, arrange some leaves on top of the cake, dust with icing sugar through a sieve, then carefully remove the leaves so that the silhouettes remain.

The Trust has many peacefully ornamental herb gardens: that at Scotney Castle in Kent is a beautiful circular space gathered round an old well head, and is full of spring-flowering bulbs as well as herbs, and Gunby Hall in Lincolnshire has a pleasing and informal mixture of lavenders and roses framed by old brick walls.

The sharp, clear scent of dried lavender from bed linen stored with lavender bags is one of the pleasantest ways of drifting off to sleep, and I try and make time every summer to sew a fresh batch of lavender bags to keep in the airing cupboard. Gather the spikes of flowers on a dry day when they are just about open; cut them with the longest stalks you can, as this helps to keep the bush in shape. Tie them together and hang them upside down to dry in a current of air. After a week or so, depending on the weather (damp air will delay the process), take them down and strip the flowers from the stalks into a paper bag. Stitch the flowers into bags made from tightly woven cotton, so that none of the lavender 'dust' can escape.

Oil of lavender was often used to treat headaches, and lavender water was considered an allowable scent for a young girl to wear. I like the following Victorian recipe for its combination of herbal wisdom and alcoholic strength:

LAVENDER DROPS

Stir as many fresh lavender flowers into a cup of brandy as the brandy will absorb. Transfer to a jar with a good lid, screw it down tightly and leave for a fortnight. Strain and add a pinch of ground cloves, then rebottle. Take 6 drops on a lump of sugar to relieve a headache, particularly a sick headache, or you can add the drops to a glass of hot water, and sweeten this with a little honey.

Cooking with lavender has gained popularity recently, with many *nouvelle cuisine* recipes suggesting combinations such as rabbit with a lavender sauce, or chicken baked in a lavender-flavoured crust. For these recipes, I think the so-called French lavender (*Lavendula stoechas*) much more suitable than our English lavender, since it has a flavour which is midway between rosemary and lavender – good with savoury dishes. But it is a tender plant and needs a warm, sunny and well-drained site. The following Edwardian recipe could use either. If using French lavender, I suggest using the vinegar for salads and sauces; if English, dilute it with still mineral water to make a refreshing toilet water for use on a hot summer's day:

LAVENDER VINEGAR

To every pint [600ml] of the best champagne vinegar put half an ounce [15g] of fresh lavender flowers and the thin rind of a lemon. Infuse for twenty-four hours in a stone jar, then take the jar and set it over hot embers to digest for ten or twelve hours. Filter and bottle the vinegar, dipping the corks in wax.

NB A stone jar isn't necessary – a Kilner jar will do just as well, and can be kept warm quite safely in a pan of hot water for the digesting time.

Another splendid National Trust herb garden is to be found at Hardwick Hall in Derbyshire, that gaunt and vainglorious house built by the redoubtable Bess of Hardwick, its cliff-like walls culminating in her initials triumphantly outlined against the sky. To complement the architecture, this garden has been planned on a large scale – huge towering stems of lovage are offset by clipped yews, and impressive columns of golden hops, trained up poles in the centre of each bed, stand in pools of golden marigolds and the sharp sword-like leaves of *Iris germanica* (or orris), all quite unlike the tranquil planting at Sissinghurst.

This recipe for a pleasant tonic makes use of hop flowers. The bitter taste is offset by the richness of the sherry.

HOP TONIC

Fill a jam-jar with dried hop flowers, gathered in September and spread on newspaper in an airing cupboard to dry. Top up the jar with dry or medium-dry sherry, according to your taste. Cap tightly and leave for three weeks. Strain well and bottle, and take a wineglassful in a little water as a tonic.

Hops are also known for their soporific effect, so the same mixture taken in hot water at bed time may help you to a sound night's sleep. Hop pillows are said to be effective against snoring; I have not found this to be so, but they certainly can make you feel drowsy. The smell of them in a stuffy bedroom is not attractive, so it is a good idea to mix them with other dried herbs that smell rather sweeter, such as lemon balm and lavender.

Marigolds (*Calendula officinalis*) are simple, bright, cheerful flowers which we now use simply as decoration, although a bunch of flowers on the kitchen table is said to absorb cooking smells and prevent them wafting through the house. But so necessary were they thought to be that Gerard describes spice sellers and grocers selling the dried petals by the pennyworth from barrels 'insomuch that no broths are well made without dried Marigolds'. Richard Bradley, in his book *The Country Housewife and Lady's Director* (1727), gives details of how to obtain the juice for colouring cheese: 'Gather your Marygold Flowers in a dry Day, and pick the golden-colour'd Leaves from them. As soon as you have pick'd a sufficient quantity of these Leaves for your use, bruise them in a Mortar – and strain out the Juice.' This juice was added to the milk at the same time as the rennet, and turned the cheese a golden colour. It must have been a laborious task, first picking enough petals from the flowers, and then squeezing out enough juice to colour the cheese. Here is a recipe which cheats a little, but reproduces the effect. It was given to me by Isabelle King, the talented young cook in the restaurant at Polesden Lacey, in Surrey:

MARIGOLD CHEESECAKE

2oz (50g) unsalted butter
4oz (125g) digestive
  biscuits, crushed
1lb (450g) curd or cream
  cheese
2oz (50g) caster sugar
few drops vanilla essence

1pt (500ml) dry measure
  fresh marigold petals
½pt (250ml) whipping
  cream
½oz (12g) gelatine
1 tablespoon (15ml)
  lemon juice

Melt the butter over a low heat and stir the biscuit crumbs into it. Spread these evenly over the base of a loose-bottomed cake tin of 8in (20cm) diameter and leave to cool. Meanwhile, beat together until smooth the curd or cream cheese and the sugar, together with a few drops of vanilla essence. Chop the marigold petals roughly, reserving a few for decoration, and fold these into the mixture. Whip the cream until it stands in soft peaks and fold that in as well. Heat the gelatine, 2 tablespoons (30ml) water and the lemon juice over a low heat until the gelatine has dissolved and stir this gently but thoroughly into the mixture. Taste the mixture, adding a little more vanilla, or lemon juice, if necessary. Pour the mixture over the crumb base and chill in the fridge until set. Decorate with the remaining marigold petals, with one marigold flower as a centrepiece.

As many 'useful' plants were grown for their flowers as for any other part, although medicinally it was often the roots which were the most efficacious. Bergamot (*Monarda didyma*) leaves make a pleasant tea, but the exotic red horned flowers make a decorative addition to salads, as do nasturtium flowers. Indeed, for centuries salads were much more adventurous than a mere combination of lettuce, cress, tomatoes and cucumber. In 1653, Gervase Markham gave a recipe for 'a good simple Sallat' of 'Samphire, Bean-cods, Sparagus, and Cucumbers, served with Oyl, Vinegar, and Pepper'. As for 'Compound Sallets', these were elaborate mixtures of 'the young Buds and Knots of all manner of wholsom Herbs, at their first springing; as red Sage, Mint, Lettice, Violets, Marigolds, Spinage and many other mixed together.' Later he suggests preserving in vinegar such things as violets, primroses, cowslips, pinks and broom flowers, in order to make a 'preserved Sallet'.

The main reason for this interest was that salads were regarded then, as now, as healthy food, but in a way that made use of medicinal herbs and their general tonic properties to a far greater extent. The various components of a salad were enlarged on to a weighty degree by John Evelyn in *Acetaria* to explain 'the Skill and Judgment requir'd, how to suit and mingle our Sallet Ingredients so as may best agree with the Constitution of the Humors of those who either stand in need of, or affect these Refreshments, and by so adjusting them, that as nothing should be suffered to domineer, so should none of them lose their genuine Gust, Savour or Vertue.'

To create a salad of the complexity of a grand sallet, it is worth exploring what plants can be grown to add interest. I have far too few violets in my garden to want to eat them, but nasturtiums (called 'scurvy-grass' in the old books, because of their valuable vitamin C content) are prolific plants, and their peppery leaves, rather more sweetly flavoured flowers and crisp seed-pods, all add interest to salads. So do radish pods which have a delicious flavour, rather milder than the radish itself; simply leave two or three radishes in the ground to flower and then go to seed. Harvest the pods when they are crisp, green and juicy, and either pickle them in vinegar, or eat them fresh, whole or sliced across into small pieces. They go well with Chinese leaves – which Evelyn would have enjoyed.

To Pickle Radish or Nasturtium Pods

Pick the pods on a dry day, rinse them under running water and dry them as thoroughly as possible. Put them into clean, dry jars, and top up with vinegar prepared in the following way. To each pint (500ml) of white wine or malt vinegar, add 1oz (25g) salt and 6 peppercorns. Bring to the boil, boil for 1 minute, then strain and cool. When cold, pour over the pods. You can always add to the jars as the pods ripen. Keep nasturtium pods for at least 6 months before eating; radish pods can be eaten within 1 month, and should not be kept too long or they will lose their crispness.

Evelyn lists 35 plants which are suitable for salading, including the exotic sounding viper's grass or Tragopogon, which is in fact salsify – 'Excellent against the Palpitation of the Heart besides a very sweet and pleasant sallet', but garlic was not included. 'We absolutely forbid it entrance into our Salleting', Evelyn thunders, suggesting another allium he calls 'Raccombo', or rocambole, instead. This is *Allium scorodoprasum*, also called Spanish garlic and now rarely found in any herb garden. Garlic chives make a good substitute, having just that combination of flavours and the additional attraction of white flower heads in the late summer.

One of the problems with this use of herbs in salad is that the same care must be taken with them as with herbal medicines. I often come across mention of rocket in salads, as being of the same variety as a pretty cottage garden plant called Sweet Rocket, or Sweet Dame's Violet. In fact, this is *Hesperis matronalis*, which has white or pale purple flowers that give out a wonderful scent in the evening, and which look lovely growing amongst old roses. Salad rocket is *Eruca sativa*, the leaves of which look rather like those of an overgrown radish and which have a somewhat similar peppery flavour; it is well worth a place in the salad garden, but not in the border.

Similar but potentially more serious mistakes can be made over bay leaves. In Victorian books these are often called 'laurel', and for some time I could not understand how anyone could mistake the narrow, oval, dull-green leaves of the bay (*Laurus nobilis*) for the much broader shiny green leaves of the laurel. But the cherry laurel (*Prunus laurocerasus*) was introduced into Britain around 1850 and became popular with cooks because the leaves had a flavour of bitter almonds. However, whereas a couple of bay leaves used to flavour a casserole can do you little harm, two laurel leaves can be poisonous, another example of how risky it can be relying on the seeming innocence of herbs as flavourings or as medicines.

Useful plants can be found tucked away in corners of many Trust gardens: at Uppark, by the Gothick summer-house grows a good patch of soapwort (*Saponaria officinalis*), which Lady Meade-Fetherstonhaugh used to clean the old and fragile textiles of the house. She describes her first introduction to the remarkable cleaning powers of this plant as a sort of witch-like initiation ceremony, watching the muslin bags containing the herb bobbing about on the surface of the 'seething spring water in the cauldron', but was amazed at its ability to ease out centuries of dirt so gently from the delicate fibres of the fabrics that she used it regularly ever after. It is a pretty plant, worth growing, and using, too. Simply infuse a handful of the leaves and stems in boiling water, then let this cool before using it for washing any delicate fabric – it is most effective.

The herb garden is always one of the pleasantest places to sit on a hot afternoon, whether it is a very formal planting kept in place by little box hedges, as at Moseley Old Hall near Wolverhampton, or at Little Moreton Hall in Cheshire, or a more unchecked gathering of large plants like monkshood and elecampane at Buckland Abbey, the Devon home of Cistercian monks in the thirteenth century and Sir Francis Drake in the sixteenth century. The aromatic scents of these medicinal and culinary herbs are very different from the heady perfumes of herbaceous plants and shrubs, and the sensation of being in a 'physic garden' full of curative properties is very strong. Just such a physic garden, covering a generous $1\frac{1}{2}$ acres, can be seen at Calke Abbey (it is currently being restored as a kitchen garden), and its size gives some indication of just how important such a garden was to the well-being of a household. I always come home to my small collection of herbs vowing to add to them in preference to allowing more space for 'useless' plants – perhaps another clump of bronze fennel instead of the phlox, to add to salads and because a decoction of the seeds, as the herbals say 'asswageth the paine of the stomacke, and wambling of the same'.

MIXED DRIED HERBS

*1oz (25g) each lemon
    thyme, winter savory,
    marjoram and basil*

*2oz (50g) parsley
1oz (25g) dried lemon
    peel*

Gather the herbs on a dry day, just before they flower. Dry them quickly in a warm airing cupboard, strip the leaves from the stalks and store them in small jars in a dark cupboard – well-washed beef and yeast extract jars are ideal for this as they exclude the light well which is important in retaining flavour.

Combine the ingredients to make a good mix for adding to casseroles, stuffings and pasta sauces. Shake together and store as above.

HERB SAUCE

An old recipe, labelled 'to keep'. Once the bottle is opened, store it in the fridge.

*1 stick fresh horseradish
2 shallots
1 sprig each winter
    savory, basil,
    marjoram, thyme,
    tarragon*

*4 cloves
juice 1 lemon
1 wineglass wine vinegar
1pt (500ml) water
1 teaspoon (5ml)
    browning (see p.104)*

Scrub the horseradish and chop it roughly, slice the shallots and put all the ingredients in a pan. Bring to the boil, reduce the heat and simmer for 5 minutes. Strain and bottle in small amounts. Good to add to gravies and soups.

HERB VINEGAR

This is Boulestin's recipe for a vinegar to add interest to salads.

Put into a large jar 2 handfuls of tarragon, 1 of chervil mixed with mustard and cress and a clove of garlic. Pour over this 3 bottles of wine vinegar, red or white. Cover and infuse for 10 days, then decant, strain and bottle and cap tightly.

Modern mustard and cress doesn't have the flavour it had in Boulestin's time (see p.74). I found watercress, land cress or Greek cress all worked better.

The Vegetable Garden

THE VEGETABLE GARDEN

LTHOUGH the greatest period for vegetable gardening was perhaps in the late nineteenth and early twentieth centuries, before the First World War ate into the great pool of labour which made such gardens possible, they really began to flourish in the middle of the eighteenth century. At this time, the growing interest in vegetables, as opposed to salad herbs and roots, meant that they were included with fruit and flowers, and grown altogether in an often substantial, walled enclosure, with vines and fruit trees trained against the sheltering walls.

Obviously, cookery books responded to the enthusiasm for increasingly sophisticated vegetables and the need to please increasingly discerning palates, and in 1747, Hannah Glasse published *The Art of Cookery made Plain and Easy.* This is a book which can be used with little alteration even today; Mrs Glasse has a lightness of touch which fits in perfectly with modern appetites, and her recipes are plain and easy.

I was particularly reminded of her style of cookery when I visited the delightful kitchen garden at Upton House. Mrs Glasse's book and the period of Upton's principal alteration probably coincided, when Robert Child was adding to the house, enlarging the lake and adding its small temple. It is not hard to imagine, if you sit on one of the strategically placed seats looking down the steep south-facing slope of this idyllically sited kitchen garden, the baskets of asparagus and 'brockely', artichokes and spinach, being carried up to the kitchens to be 'dressed' according to methods similar to those which Mrs Glasse gives in her book:

TO DRESS GREENS, ROOTS &C.

Always be very careful that your Greens be nicely pick'd and wash'd. You should lay them in a clean Pan for fear of Sand or Dust, which is apt to hang round wooden Vessels. Boil all your Greens in a Copper sauce-pan by themselves with a great Quantity of Water.

She and I part company here – nowadays, we prefer to cook greens with as little water as possible, even steaming them, because we know rather more about vitamins than she did. On the other hand, she advocates cooking potatoes with 'as little water as you can without burning the Sauce-pan' – a risky business.

Her recipe for fried potatoes is interesting and good, and makes a wonderful accompaniment to thick slices of home-cooked ham. It is a method which dates from earlier recipes, when almost all root vegetables were treated as sweet rather than savoury dishes:

SWEET FRIED POTATOES

1½ lb (675g) potatoes, scrubbed, boiled in their skins, peeled and sliced fairly thinly
oil or fat for frying

4 tablespoons (60ml) medium dry sherry
1 tablespoon (15ml) demerara sugar

Heat a heavy frying pan, add a thin layer of oil, and when this has heated, add the potatoes; these precautions should help to prevent the potatoes sticking. Let them fry over a medium heat for about 10 minutes or until they have developed a good crust on the bottom. Put a large plate over the frying pan and tip the pan so that the potatoes land upside down on the plate. Add a little more oil or fat to the pan and slide the potatoes back in, to cook on the other side for another 10 minutes. Slide on to a heated dish to serve, sprinkling them with the sugar and sherry.

ASPARAGUS PEAS

Asparagus was often served as 'sprue peas', a method which appeals very much today when asparagus is expensive. It consisted of cutting the stalks of thin, green 'sprue' asparagus into small pieces about the size of a pea, and cooking them in the same manner. They take slightly longer than new peas, and I found it best to cook the pieces from the lower end of the stalks first, adding the tips last so that they shouldn't overcook. Some recipes reserve the tips for another dish, or for a garnish. Cooked this way, asparagus makes a perfect accompaniment to lamb, chicken and fish; it is a method which deserves revival.

Spring Soup

Typical of recipes of this period, this is a good way of making use of a small quantity of asparagus and peas at the beginning of the season. It is a soup which was often listed as 'without meat', especially for fast days, which makes it suitable for modern vegetarians.

large bunch asparagus –	*1 teaspoon (5ml) sugar*
about 1lb (450g)	*2pt (1.25l) vegetable*
½lb (225g) spinach	*stock or water*
half a large cucumber	*1lb (450g) fresh peas in*
2oz (50g) butter	*their pods, or 6–8oz*
bunch spring onions	*(175–225g) shelled*
salt and pepper	*weight*

Cut off the asparagus tips and set these aside, together with 2 tablespoons of peas. Clean the asparagus stalks and remove the tough ends, slice the rest into ½ in (1.25cm) pieces. Wash and chop the spinach roughly, peel and dice the cucumber, trim and slice the spring onions. Melt the butter in a heavy pan, add all the vegetables except the reserved asparagus tips and peas. Stir well and cook, covered, over a low heat for 15 minutes. Add a little salt and pepper, a teaspoonful of sugar and the stock or water and cook for another 15–20 minutes or until the asparagus stalks are very soft. While the soup is cooking, steam the asparagus tips and the reserved peas until tender. Purée the soup through a sieve or food–mill to remove any fibres and return to the rinsed-out pan. Check the seasoning and reheat with the asparagus tips and peas. This is not a thick soup, but if you feel it needs extra body, add a tablespoon of cornflour mixed with a little water to thicken it. Serve with croutons.

Another recipe typical of this light, fresh approach to vegetables is Mrs Glasse's broccoli salad:

Brockely in Sallad

Brockely is a pretty Dish, by way of Sallad in the Middle of a Table. Boil it like Asparagus, lay it in your Dish, and beat up Oil and Vinegar, and a little Salt. Garnish round with Stertion-buds.

NB Nasturtium buds add just the right touch of bright colour, as well as a peppery flavour which goes well with the broccoli.

The next recipe is good to serve with a light meat such as chicken or spring lamb, and equally good as a meal in itself accompanied by buttery new potatoes. It is another of Mrs Glasse's.

A RAGOO OF BEANS WITH A FORCE
or French Beans with a Carrot Purée

4 large carrots (old ones give the best flavour)
1oz (25g) butter
2 egg yolks
salt and freshly ground pepper

1lb (450g) French beans, topped and tailed and broken into 1in (2.5cm) pieces
½pt (250ml) light stock
3 tablespoons (45ml) browning (see p.104)

Peel the carrots thinly, cook them in as little water as possible, or steam, drain and purée with the butter. When they have cooled a little, beat in the egg yolks, and season. Butter 4 small ovenproof ramekins and divide the carrot mixture between them. Meanwhile, blanch the beans in boiling salted water for 2 minutes, drain them and return to the pan with the stock and the browning to finish cooking. Bake the carrot ramekins in a hot oven (400°F, 200°C; gas mark 6) for 15 minutes, until they are puffy and beginning to crisp round the edges. Turn each out on to a warmed plate and surround with the beans, which should have just enough liquid with them to moisten. Serve at once, decorated with a sprig of chervil or parsley.

If serving as a vegetable, bake the carrot purée in one dish, turn it out on to a flat serving platter and surround it with the beans.

VEGETABLE STOCK

Many Georgian vegetable dishes were served in a brown sauce, rather than the white sauce that became synonymous with vegetables in the inter-war years. This does not necessarily mean using a meat-based stock to achieve this, and there were plenty of vegetable stock recipes in order to avoid having to serve meat during such times as Lent. These were usually a combination of root vegetables, sliced onions and plenty of flavouring herbs such as thyme, chervil, parsley, lovage or celery, together with the skins of onions to give a good brown colour, simmered together, then strained and seasoned.

The kitchen garden at Felbrigg is another fine example of an eighteenth-century garden. Here Mr Bullock, the head gardener, has a vegetable plot, orchard, glasshouse (which grows Black Hamburg grapes) and herb border, as well as wall-trained apples, pears, peaches, plums and, as he says, 'in a good year, figs'. There is also a fine octagonal dovecote which must have supplied the house with a considerable amount of food, since there are spaces for about 2,000 birds. While their manure must have been invaluable for the garden, their instinct to attack vegetables must have been difficult to control. This old recipe is an indication of rough justice: pigeons are now readily available in good supermarkets.

COMPÔTE OF PIGEONS AND PEAS

*2 thick slices of
    unsmoked bacon
4 oven-ready pigeons
    (one per person)
lard or dripping
2 tablespoons (30ml)
    flour
1½pt (750ml) stock*

*a good bunch of fresh
    herbs – bay, parsley,
    thyme, marjoram and
    a sage leaf
12oz (350g) peas, shelled
    weight
salt and freshly ground
    pepper*

Cut the bacon into small cubes, cover these with cold water in a small saucepan and bring to the boil; drain immediately and put them into a sauté pan over a medium heat until they begin to sizzle and release their fat. Season the pigeons and add them to the bacon pieces, browning them all over – add a little lard or dripping if there isn't enough fat from the bacon.

Transfer both pigeons and bacon pieces to a casserole with a close-fitting lid. Stir flour into the fat in the pan. Pour on the hot stock, bring it to the boil, stirring in all the pieces which have stuck to the bottom and which will add flavour to the dish. Pour over the pigeons, tuck the bunch of herbs down amongst them, cover tightly and simmer gently for 20 minutes. Raise the heat a little and add the peas. Bring the liquid back to simmering point, cover and simmer gently for a further 20 minutes, or until the birds are tender. Dish them up on to a shallow platter, surrounded by the peas and bits of bacon. Reduce the stock left in the casserole by fast boiling until you have about ½ pint (250ml) left, check the seasoning and serve separately in a sauce boat. For a truly eighteenth-century touch, garnish the dish with triangular croutons of fried bread and slices of lemon with the peel nicked at intervals so that they look rather like the cogs of a clock.

Katherine Windham, wife of William Windham I of Felbrigg, collected a number of recipes into a book called *A Booke of Cookery and Housekeeping*, dated 1707; she lived at Felbrigg for 60 years, keeping house for her son Ashe after the death of her husband in 1689. There are numerous recipes for pickling and preserving vegetables, a good recipe for 'My Sons Rice Puding', in which she sensibly observes that 'it is best to boyle the Milke and Rice together first'. Her recipe 'To Fry Cucumbers' gives an indication that these vegetables were being grown in the kitchen garden at that time. They would have been grown under bell-glasses, forced on a hotbed of earth and dung; details for growing them in this way appear in many gardening books of the period, such as John Hill's *Compleat Body of Gardening*.

Cucumber makes an excellent hot vegetable, and is far more digestible when cooked than raw. Here is Katherine Windham's recipe, with my own adaptation underneath. In deference to today's lighter eating habits, I omit the thickening to the sauce; it is just as good without. It makes a very good accompaniment to poached chicken, or to any fish dish.

KATHERINE WINDHAM'S CUCUMBER DISH

Slice them but not too thin, fry them in Butter and strain them from it, make a Browning and put in a little Gravy and let them stew gently for an hour, put in a little peper and salt, and as you send it in squeeze in $\frac{1}{2}$ a Lemon.

1oz (25g) butter	*salt and freshly ground*
2 slim cucumbers	*pepper*
$\frac{1}{2}$pt (250ml) light stock	*lemon juice*
(fish, or chicken,	
according to the dish it	
is to accompany)	

Melt the butter in a heavy, wide pan. Peel the cucumbers and slice them lengthways, remove as many of the seeds as you can, then slice them fairly thickly. Toss the slices in the butter, put a lid on the pan and let them stew for about 5 minutes. Heat the stock and pour it over the cucumbers, just enough to cover them. Cover the pan, and let them simmer very gently until they are tender and the stock slightly reduced. Season and add just enough lemon juice to sharpen the flavour.

The elegant and dramatic shapes of globe artichokes and their near relations, the cardoons, gave extra decorative value to vegetable gardens. While the artichoke has remained popular, the cardoon has all but vanished, probably because it needs blanching and earthing up in the winter which the artichoke does not. On the day I visited the walled vegetable garden at Barrington Court, there were some splendidly opulent artichokes ready for eating, and these vegetables add to the stately beauty of the kitchen gardens at Upton House and West Green, too. For those who grow their own, the following recipe is very useful since it makes use of the immature heads which are best removed in order to produce large and meaty heads later on.

To Fry Small Suckers of Artichokes, or Small Artichokes

Gather the young Heads of Artichokes, and boil them with Salt and Water till they are tender; these Artichokes should be no bigger than middling Apples; split these in four or six Parts each, flower them well, and fry them crisp in Hogs-lard, and eat them with Butter, Pepper, and a little Verjuice or Orange-juice.

NB Drain the cooked artichokes thoroughly before cutting them into quarters, and then put them into a paper bag together with seasoned flour. Shake well to coat them all over, then deep fry in sunflower oil (rather than lard) until crisp. They are very good indeed, as they have no thistly chokes at this stage.

For anyone with blanched cardoon stems available, the above method works well, cutting the stalks into 2in (5cm) long pieces and steaming or boiling them in salted water until tender, then flouring and deep-frying in the same way. Alternatively simmer them in a little stock and butter until tender, and add a spoonful or two of browning (p.104) or herb sauce (p.30) to finish.

Most old recipes for artichokes use the bases, for adding to pies and to sauces, rather as we might make use of mushrooms today. There are plenty of recipes for drying and pickling them, to ensure a year-round supply of these obviously useful vegetables.

It interested me to find that these early gardens included vegetables with which we have become familiar only over the past few years, but which had disappeared for many years in between. In *The Country Housewife and Lady's Director*, Richard Bradley quotes 'C.B. A Gentlewoman in Suffolk' who gives details of 'The Gourmandine Pea', which is described exactly as the mange-tout pea, even giving a suggestion for stir-frying them together with 'Mutton Steaks'. C.B. also mentions the sugar pea as being a superior variation, 'being somewhat sweeter than the former, and Pod fuller of Pulp'.

Upton, Felbrigg, even West Green, represent eighteenth-century vegetable gardening at its best, but vegetable gardens were set to become larger, perhaps less decorative but certainly more productive. As large sums of money began to be made from industry, larger and larger houses were built with the proceeds. These establishments required formidable numbers of staff; comforts such as fires in the bedrooms and endless hot water for washing – the sort of luxuries which the earlier inhabitants of Upton and Felbrigg might have thought unnecessary – the Victorians and Edwardians found vital to their well-being and to that of their guests.

To feed so many, vegetable gardens, orchards, hot-houses and hot walls were equally necessary. The undisciplined mixture of vegetables and herbs disappeared and was replaced by the regimented rows of lettuce, carrots and leeks which can look equally pleasing, though less romantic. These horticultural factories were placed some way away from the house (perhaps, in a primmer age, to keep young gardeners well away from the young girls working in the house) rather than as an adjunct to the main garden as they had been in the previous century.

Such a siting is obvious at Calke Abbey where a walk uphill from the house, through the Trust's newly restored Pleasure Ground, takes you into a different world. The main kitchen garden, reached through a small walled garden filled with a brightly coloured, highly scented and ornate scheme of bedding-out plants, extends over a huge 4½-acre area presided over by a splendid conservatory where presumably house guests could sit and watch the industry of such a garden. This vegetable garden is now a paddock, too large an area to maintain without a huge workforce, and the conservatory is in ruins, although with plans for its renovation. But leading out of this garden is the smaller physic garden, once used for medicinal herbs, and this is now being restored as the vegetable garden. Old varieties of vegetables are being grown there, and the produce once again sent down to the house; Mr Biggins, the gardener in charge of the Trust's restoration of the garden, told me that he was amazed how quickly his contributions to the restaurant were consumed. No wonder 4 acres were needed to feed such a large house fully occupied.

The heyday of Calke was during the short lifetime of Sir George Crewe. From 1819 until his early death at the age of 48 in 1844, he proved himself to be of a different mould from his shy and reclusive father, Sir Henry, setting the estate and the house to rights, entering into the politics of the county, and entertaining, although never lavishly.

The following soup is one which might well have been served at Calke during those days. It is economical, and makes use of the products of a prolific vegetable garden, but is sophisticated enough, with its flavour of curry (curry powder and paste had entered English cooking not many years before), not to seem too provincial:

VEGETABLE MULLIGATAWNY SOUP

1½oz (37g) butter
1 large mild onion
1lb (450g) courgettes or
   young marrow
1 small cucumber
2 eating apples, of a
   fairly acid variety

1 dessertspoon (10ml)
   mild curry powder
salt
about 2pt (1.25l) stock or
   water

Melt the butter in a heavy pan, add the peeled and chopped onion, courgettes or marrow (if using the latter, remove the seeds), and cucumber, and the peeled, cored and diced apple.

Let them stew gently in the butter, stirring from time to time, for about 15 minutes. Add the curry powder and about 1 teaspoon (5ml) salt, then pour on enough stock just to cover the vegetables. Simmer until all are soft, then liquidise the contents of the pan. Return to the rinsed-out pan and add enough stock to bring the quantity up to 2 pints. Reheat until very hot and check the seasoning – a squeeze of lemon juice may be added at this stage if the apples were very sweet.

On a more modern note, this soup is very good served chilled, with a garnish of fresh, chopped, coriander.

The following recipe, for little rolls filled with a mushroom mixture, would probably have formed one of the dozen or more dishes that constituted one 'course' at any dinner until the time that *service à la Russe* came in at the end of the nineteenth century, and at which servants, waiting at table, would hand the food to each individual guest. Before that, guests helped themselves to the dishes, and probably made rather a mess of them. As the dishes stayed on the table throughout the course, anything that remained looking neat and tidy must have been very desirable.

MUSHROOM LOAVES

4 brown rolls (miniature brown loaves are perfect for this)
sunflower oil
12oz (350g) button mushrooms
1oz (25g) butter

1 tablespoon (15ml) cornflour
scant ½pt (250ml) single cream
salt and pepper
grating of nutmeg
squeeze of lemon juice
4 bay leaves

Slice the tops off the rolls or loaves, reserve them and scoop out the crumb carefully. With a little sunflower oil, brush the inside of each roll and the outside crust of each top slice, and arrange them on a baking sheet. Put them to crisp in an oven preheated to 300°F, 150°C; gas mark 2 while you prepare the mushroom mixture. Slice the mushrooms thinly and cook them gently in the butter until tender. Stir the cornflour into the cream and add this to the mushrooms in the pan, stirring over a gentle heat for a minute or two. Season with salt and pepper, the nutmeg and a little lemon juice to bring out the flavours. Fill each warm, crisp roll with the mixture, place the tops on, slightly askew, and garnish each with a bayleaf at a jaunty angle, rather like a feather in a cap.

These make an excellent starter, but are also good cold, as picnic food. If serving them in this way, cool the crisped rolls on a rack and store in an airtight box; spoon in the cold mushroom mixture as nearly as possible to serving time.

Quarry Bank Mill at Styal is one of the Trust's few industrial properties. An elegant eighteenth-century cotton mill set deep in a river valley, it hardly fulfils most people's idea of an industrial landscape, but it was placed here to take advantage of the power offered by the River Bollin. To house the workforce the mill's owners, the Greg family, built first an Apprentice House and then an entire village, each cottage having enough land to enable the cottagers to grow their own vegetables. The village is still owned by the Trust, and is largely inhabited by people who can trace their ancestry right back to those early mill workers who came to Styal as apprentices in the 1820s.

Less land is used in the village for growing vegetables now as most people prefer to concentrate on flowers – the autumn gardens are bright with dahlias and chrysanthemums. But the garden at the Apprentice House, restored to give some idea of the life of the young workforce, is a perfect example of vegetable growing at its simplest. There are no orangeries here, or hot-beds, or glasshouses. Instead, a series of small, neat beds, each with its rows of carrots and leeks, potatoes and kale, indicate the simple but wholesome diet which the children helped to produce. It is now presided over by Mrs Brittan, who, over the last five years, has painstakingly developed the site and researched into the varieties of vegetables and fruit which grew here. I was lucky enough to live at Styal for ten years, and to watch and share in Pat's triumphs and disasters, such as the rediscovery of the local Withington Welter apple, and the trying out of some of the old varieties of potatoes. Old isn't always good, and when scraping the burnt remains of Edzel Blue potatoes off the bottom of the saucepan, where they had disintegrated to a shapeless glue, you could see why they hadn't survived to this day. But other vegetables, such as Ragged Jack kale and Painted Lady runner beans, are well worth growing and it is good to see that they are just beginning to make their way back into the seed catalogues.

Recipes which come to mind here have little or nothing to do with sophisticated entertaining. Here, vegetables were used to feed hungry children, and to give them sufficient energy to carry out a good day's work, followed by a long evening's education, insisted upon by their strict but philanthropic employers.

Mutton Broth

1½lb (675g) scrag end of   1 large carrot
   mutton, cut into pieces   ¼ small turnip
2 teaspoons (10ml) salt   1½oz (37g) pearl barley
1 stick celery   1 teaspoon (5ml)
1 onion   chopped parsley

Mutton gives by far the best flavour for this broth, but is
sadly not easy to come by. If you can't get it, ask for hogget
(two-year-old lamb), or use 2lb (900g) scrag of lamb. Put the
meat into a large pan and cover it with 2½ pints (1.5l) cold
water. Bring slowly to boil, skimming off any froth as it rises,
then, when it begins to boil, add 2 teaspoons (10ml) salt and
the celery and onion, reduce the heat and simmer very
gently, either on top of the stove or in a low oven, for
2 hours. If possible, take the soup off the heat, leave overnight
until cold, and lift off the fat which will have solidified on the
top. If not, then skim off as much surface fat as possible.
Remove the celery and onion, and lift out the meat. Cut the
best chunks of meat into small pieces and return them to the
broth. Cut the carrot and turnip into thin strips and add them
to the soup, together with the pearl barley. Simmer for
another half an hour or until the new ingredients are tender,
check the seasoning and add the parsley. Serve very hot, with
plenty of good crusty bread.

A similarly nourishing but basic recipe follows, called simply a
Vegetable Pudding. It is excellent, and worth trying, especially as
it has the advantage of being a vegetable dish which needs no last
minute attention. It is good with roast lamb, or a beef casserole.

Vegetable Pudding

1lb (450g) floury   1 small onion, finely
   potatoes   chopped
8oz (225g) carrots,   3 eggs
   peeled and diced   salt and pepper
4oz (125g) turnip,   chopped parsley
   peeled and diced

Scrub the potatoes and boil until done. Leave to cool a little.
Steam the carrots and turnip. Mash the cooked vegetables
together and mix in the onion and the beaten eggs, then
season generously. Butter a 2-pint (1.25l) pudding basin and
put the mixture into it, cover the top with greaseproof paper

and foil and steam for an hour. Turn out and dust with chopped parsley. This pudding can also be baked in the oven, in a buttered pie dish, with butter dotted over the top. Cook for about 45 minutes in a moderate oven (375°F, 190°C; gas mark 5) until the top is brown.

Lanhydrock House, a great grey pile comfortably situated in the green and sheltered valley of the River Fowey in Cornwall, no longer has a vegetable garden. It does, however, have the most wonderfully complete series of kitchens, sculleries, dairies, bakehouses and larders, all equipped to make what must have been one of the best set of kitchen quarters in late Victorian England. The scullery boasts a special coal range for cooking vegetables and deep, lead-lined sinks in which to prepare them. The dishes devised here, to the highest standards of *haute cuisine* by a chef and his retinue who travelled between the Robartes' London house, Wimpole Hall near Cambridge (also owned by the Trust), and Lanhydrock, owed much to the influence of Charles Elmé Francatelli. Francatelli was at one time Chief Cook-in-Ordinary to Queen Victoria; he was of Italian extraction, educated in France and trained by the legendary Carême. His two books *The Modern Cook* and *The Cook's Guide* (of which a copy survives at Lanhydrock) set a pattern for formal, lengthy and copious menus which was not to change until the First World War.

Francatelli's Italian Salad

Many of Francatelli's recipes are extremely elaborate; his salads contain as many ingredients as those of John Evelyn, with the important exception that most of the vegetable ingredients are cooked first – at this stage of English cookery, cooked vegetables were considered far healthier than raw ones. His recipe for Italian salad contains cauliflower, asparagus tips, French beans, new potatoes, beetroot, artichoke bottoms and peas, all set in aspic in a ring mould, then turned out and filled with more cooked vegetables mixed with a vinaigrette to which more aspic was added.

A 'Chartreuse' of vegetables was another elaborate confection to be found on the dining-tables of rich Victorians. Francatelli gives a recipe for one in which the mould was lined with a mosaic of 'tiles' cut from carrots and turnips. This was filled with a mixture of partridge meat layered with cooked savoy cabbage moistened with a brown sauce. All ingredients having been cooked before their arrangement in the mould, the whole only needed to be steamed to rewarm it before being turned out, garnished and served hot. It is a delicious recipe, but the flavours are essentially those of a very simple rustic dish – braised game birds served on a bed of cabbage and root vegetables; however, such simplicity did not appeal at that period (although I am sure the robust flavours appealed strongly to country appetites) so the whole thing needed disguising and presenting in a much more refined manner.

Tomato recipes were finding their way into most recipe books at this period, tomatoes having been regarded with some suspicion for long after their first appearance in the gardens of England. This might have been because they had been christened 'love-apples'; until the nineteenth century, most vegetables were considered to be aphrodisiacs when first introduced into this country, which therefore precluded their being presented to polite society. The following recipe, for 'Tomatas, à la Provençale' is one of Francatelli's simpler creations.

TOMATOES À LA PROVENÇALE

4 large beef tomatoes
2 shallots, finely chopped
6 tablespoons (90ml)
  olive or sunflower oil
4oz (125g) button
  mushrooms

1oz (25g) parsley, finely
  chopped
2oz (50g) cooked ham,
  finely diced
pinch dried thyme
salt and pepper
dried breadcrumbs

Remove a slice from the top of each tomato and scoop out the insides. Cook the chopped shallots until soft and golden in a little of the olive oil, then add the mushrooms, parsley, ham, thyme and seasonings. Cook all together, stirring from time to time, over a medium heat. Stuff the tomatoes with this mixture. Put the rest of the oil into a gratin dish and arrange the tomatoes in it, sprinkle the breadcrumbs over the top and bake for 20 minutes in a hot over (400°F, 200°C; gas mark 6), until the tomatoes are soft and the tops crisp. This is also good as a cold dish.

The following recipe is one of Mrs Beeton's and is one of many in the later editions of her famous *Book of Household Management*. It is very good, and simple, useful to keep on hand in the fridge or freezer for serving with Indian dishes, for adding to pasta sauces or for eating with cold meats.

Tomatoes Chow-chow

6 large ripe tomatoes	2 tablespoons (30ml)
1 large onion	brown sugar
1 green pepper	2 teacupfuls (about $\frac{1}{2}$pt
1 tablespoon (15ml)	or 250ml) wine
salt	vinegar

Peel and cut fine the tomatoes, chop fine the onion and pepper, add the salt, sugar, and vinegar. Stew gently for one hour.

After the First World War, the labour-intensive recipes such as those to be found in the pages of cookery writers like Francatelli no longer appealed to households with dwindling resources. Staff were harder to find, and harder to keep, and English country-house cookery began to slide downhill, at least as far as vegetables were concerned. Kitchen gardens had to manage with fewer staff, the lads who performed the lowly tasks of weeding and pricking out had gone to war and all too often had not returned. In the hands of the inexperienced cook, Mrs Beeton's *Book of Household Management* was a dangerous weapon. Her instruction for boiling vegetables with '1 heaped tablespoonful of salt to each half gallon of water', plus a bit of soda for green vegetables to keep them green (in fact, the Romans used nitre, potassium nitrate, for the same effect), resulted in the famous English dishes of boiled watery cabbage, or boiled watery sprouts, or boiled watery carrots, perpetuated by those who did not understand that it wasn't necessary to use 4 pints (2.5l) of water to cook a cabbage, or half-a-dozen carrots.

But the rationing of the Second World War revived interest in vegetables and their production. Kitchen gardens were brought back into use; Margaret Meade-Fetherstonhaugh writes of the gardens at Uppark winning prizes for their 'fruit, vegetables, honey and figs'. At this time, Constance Spry wrote a charming and very useful cookery book called *Come into the Garden, Cook*, published in 1942. It gives a good idea of how to make best use of garden produce to eke out any luxuries which existed in the form of butter or eggs or meat. Her recipe for 'Pain de Legumes' – a light steamed soufflé – is one which I have adapted many times. Wartime or not, it makes good vegetarian food, and this is my version.

STEAMED SPINACH SOUFFLÉ
WITH TOMATO SAUCE

1½lb (675g) raw spinach,
cooked, drained and
puréed
2oz (50g) margarine or
butter

1oz (25g) stale
breadcrumbs
4 tablespoons (60ml) hot
milk
salt, pepper and nutmeg
2 egg yolks

For the sauce

½ onion, diced
½ carrot, diced
2 tablespoons (30ml)
olive oil
2lb (900g) fresh
tomatoes, skinned and
chopped, or 2 tins
chopped tomatoes

2 cloves garlic
bunch of herbs – bayleaf,
parsley, marjoram and
thyme
salt and pepper
sugar

To make the soufflé, put the spinach purée in a pan with the butter or margarine, over a low heat until the butter melts. Soak the breadcrumbs in the hot milk, then sieve them into the spinach mixture, together with a seasoning of salt, pepper and a grating of nutmeg. Off the heat, add the beaten egg yolks. Put the mixture into a well-greased soufflé dish or, if you have one, a ring-mould. Stand this in a baking tin and add hot water to come half-way up the soufflé dish or ring-mould. Steam for about 45 minutes in the oven, set at 350°F, 180°C; gas mark 4.

While it cooks, make the sauce. Sweat the onion and carrot in the olive oil over a low heat for about 10 minutes, then add the tomatoes, garlic, herbs and a light seasoning of salt and pepper. Simmer gently with the lid off the pan until the carrot is thoroughly cooked, remove the herbs and purée the sauce. Return to the heat, check the seasoning and add sugar to taste.

Turn the soufflé out carefully on to a warmed plate and pour the tomato sauce over it.

The Orchard

THE ORCHARD

I N 1734 Richard Bradley described his ideal orchard: 'Let two Thirds at least bear Apples, and the Remainder be allotted for Pears, Plumbs, Cherries, and a Mulberry-Tree or two. The Ground thus planted may be fenced about with Hedges of Filberds and Barberries, to make it still the more compleat and delightful.' The National Trust has, over the years, followed his advice. Many properties boast orchards which are not only delightful to look at and walk in, but are fine collections of old varieties of fruit, usually historically aligned to the date of the house and indigenous to the area. This work in propagating old varieties is especially valuable since numerous old orchards have been destroyed, either by disease, or by gales, or simply in favour of modern cultivars – disease-resistant, often flavourless, but much more profitable. Many an old apple tree in many a private garden has died, only to be replaced, if at all, by one of the more readily available new varieties.

This attention to local, as well as to old varieties, has resulted in a particularly interesting collection of apples at Nunnington Hall in Ryedale, where varieties local to the dale itself, such as Burrknot, Green Balsam and Gooseberry, were planted about six years ago and are flourishing. At the restaurant here, a fine apple and elderberry tart is served to customers for Sunday lunch, making use of the freezer to make the apple and the elderberry season coincide – an advantage not given to the seventeenth-century Nunnington cooks. The elderberries are picked when black from the hedgerow trees, washed and strigged and then frozen. The mixture of flavours is a little like that of blackberry and apple.

NUNNINGTON APPLE & ELDERBERRY TART

1lb (450g) cooking apples, peeled, cored and sliced	2oz (50g) lard
	2oz (50g) soft margarine
	4oz (125g) plain flour
sugar to taste	4oz (125g) self-raising
2–4oz (50–125g) elder-	flour
berries, fresh or frozen	iced water to mix

Cook the apples in a very little water until soft, then add sufficient sugar to sweeten. Place the elderberries in a sieve to wash them, or to remove the ice particles if using frozen ones. Make up the pastry by rubbing the fat into the flour and adding iced water to mix to a soft dough. Roll out half and use it to line an 8in (20cm) pie plate, put in the apple and spread the elderberries over the top. Roll out the remaining pastry and cover the fruit, wet edges and seal firmly. Place the tart on a heated baking sheet in a hot oven (400°F, 200°C; gas mark 6) and bake for about 20 minutes, until the crust is golden. Sprinkle with caster sugar and serve hot, warm or cold, with good thick cream.

Fruit was an important component of the sweetmeats popular in Tudor England; apple, plum and quince 'pastes', more like today's fruit pastilles, were cut into shapes and rolled in sugar, and kept throughout the winter. Such reductions of fruit require plenty of raw material, so it is not surprising that numerous fruit trees were included in the garden schemes of many houses, whether or not they were planted in the sort of orchards that Richard Bradley describes. At Canons Ashby, near Daventry in Northampton-shire, the trees are planted on shallow terraces below the south front of the house, overlooking a gentle and tranquil landscape which has not changed much since the house was first built for John Dryden in the middle of the sixteenth century. The species of fruit trees now growing are those which were known to have been grown in the sixteenth century, some of them listed amongst seeds found on the *Mary Rose*, with names as romantic as their provenance – Haute Bonte, Chataigner, Virgoleuse and Scarlet Crofton.

TESTING FOR RIPENESS
A contemporary book gives the following directions on how 'to know if Apples or Pears are ripe, take one from the Middle of the Tree, cut it in the Middle, and if there be a great Hollowness and the Kernels seem loose, they are ripe'.

The following recipe is reminiscent of the almond soups of the seventeenth and eighteenth century, but the addition of the apples gives it a twentieth-century lightness. It is served in the restaurant at Blickling Hall, in Norfolk, home of the Blickling Pear, recommended by the horticulturalist Edward Bunyard in 1920.

APPLE & ALMOND SOUP

2oz (50g) butter
1 onion, finely chopped
2 sticks celery, finely
    chopped
2oz (50g) flour
2pt (1.25l) vegetable or
    chicken stock

2 cooking apples, peeled,
    cored and finely
    chopped
1oz (25g) flaked
    almonds
$\frac{1}{2}$pt (250ml) milk
seasoning
juice of half a lemon

Melt the butter, add the onion and celery and cook gently until translucent. Stir in the flour, then gradually add the heated stock, the apples and almonds. Season lightly and simmer for half an hour. Heat the milk and add it to the soup, check the seasoning and sharpen the flavour with as much lemon juice as necessary.

Erddig has another notable collection of fruit trees planted by the Trust in accordance with the basic plan of the early eighteenth-century gardens there. Some are planted as wall fruit, but most of the apples are grown as free-standing orchard trees, trained to a pyramid shape so that the effect is one of formality rather than rusticity. The wall-trained pears and apples look splendid in autumn, with the russets and reds of the fruit matching the bricks of the walls behind them – a glorious sight worth seeing before the property closes in the middle of October. This recipe is not a refined product of the eighteenth century, but a traditional Welsh one from the Lleyn Peninsula further to the west of Erddig and one which might well have been eaten in the comfortable kitchen of the house.

APPLE & POTATO PIE

1lb (450g) cooked
    potatoes
2oz (50g) butter
½oz (12g) sugar
pinch nutmeg

4oz (125g) flour
1lb (450g) well-
    flavoured dessert
    apples

Mash the potatoes while still hot with the butter and season with the sugar and nutmeg. Work in as much flour as is necessary to make a dough which can be rolled out thickly, into two rounds of which one should be about ½in (1.25cm) larger than the other. Put the smaller circle on to a well-greased baking sheet and cover with a thick layer of peeled and sliced apple. Put the larger circle on the top, pinch the edges together and cut a cross on the top to let the steam escape. Bake for about 40 minutes, or until the pastry is golden brown, in a fairly hot oven (375°F, 190°C; gas mark 5). Serve with plenty of cream.

On a more modest scale, the orchard at Hardy's Cottage in Dorset has also had new trees of old varieties added to it by the Trust. The cottage was Thomas Hardy's birthplace, and he lived there until he was 34. In his poem 'Domicilium', he describes it thus:

> It faces west, and round the back and sides
> High beeches, bending, hang a veil of boughs,
> And sweep against the roof. Wild honeysucks
> Climb on the walls, and seem to sprout a wish
> (If we may fancy wish of trees and plants)
> To overtop the apple-trees hard by.

The following recipe is for Mrs Thomas Hardy's apple jelly, for which she particularly recommended using Keswick 'codlings' (an old variety which is now being grown in the garden of the Apprentice House at Styal), an early ripening, acid and white-fleshed cooking apple.

MRS THOMAS HARDY'S APPLE JELLY

Wash apples and remove all specks. Halve and quarter them, and place in the stewpan with a little water. Boil to a pulp. Rub through hair sieve to remove all cores and rinds. To each pint of pulp allow 1lb of refined sugar. Add the finely chopped rind of a lemon with a few cloves. Boil for about ½ hour.

At Berrington Hall in Herefordshire, the newly planted orchard forms another large collection of apples – 50 different varieties of which almost half are indigenous to the area, and all date from before the beginning of this century. Trerice has another fine collection of local apples, as does Hardwick Hall, where the beautiful orchard contains varieties such as Duke of Devonshire, Norfolk Beefing and Red Bramley· (our best-known cooking apple, Bramley's Seedling, was raised at nearby Southwell, in Nottinghamshire). The Trust's work on fruit trees, tracing old varieties and growing them on, is vital to the conservation of hundreds of kinds which would otherwise disappear completely.

Many are the recipes in old cookery books for a dish called 'Black Caps', a delicious method of baking apples which has inexplicably fallen from favour and deserves revival. The apples are sprinkled thickly with sugar before being baked in a hot oven when the sugar caramelises and forms 'black' caps.

Black Caps

soft butter
4 large apples, halved
 horizontally and cored
juice and grated rind of
 1 lemon, separated

2 tablespoons (30ml)
 orange-flower water
3oz (75g) caster sugar

Butter a shallow, ovenproof dish and arrange the apples in it, cut sides down. Pour the lemon juice and orange-flower water round them, add the grated lemon rind, and sprinkle the sugar thickly over the tops of the apples. Add a couple of tablespoons of water (30ml) if the apples are large or the lemon very small. Bake for $\frac{1}{2}$ hour in a hot oven (425°F, 220°C; gas mark 7), until the sugar has caramelised and the apples are soft.

Another excellent apple recipe comes from Mrs Raffald's *The Experienced English Housekeeper*, first published in 1769. Called 'Apple Floating Island', it is a particularly light and delicate pudding, ideal for a dinner party:

To make an Apple Floating Island. Bake six or eight very large apples, when they are cold peel and core them, rub the pulp through a sieve with the back of a wooden-spoon then beat it up light with fine sugar, well sifted, to your taste; beat the whites of four eggs with orange-flower water in another bowl till it is a light froth, then mix it with your apples a little at a time till all is beat together, and exceeding light; make a rich boiled custard, and put it in a China or glass dish, and lay the apples all over it.

A MODERN APPLE FLOATING ISLAND

6 large Bramley apples
1 teaspoon (5ml) orange-
   flower water
vanilla sugar to taste

4 eggs, separated
3oz (75g) caster sugar
1pt (500ml) milk

Bake the apples in the oven until soft, cool, then peel them and remove the cores. Either push through a sieve or purée them in a food processor, then add the orange-flower water and vanilla sugar to the purée. Whisk the egg whites as for a meringue, adding half the sugar, and fold this into the apple mixture. Set aside. To make the custard, beat the egg yolks in a large bowl with the remaining sugar, and heat the milk to boiling point. Pour a little milk on to the egg yolks and beat well, then add the rest of the milk. Return this custard to the pan and, stirring continuously, cook over a low heat until the mixture thickens enough to coat the back of the spoon. Pour the custard into a shallow dish and leave it to cool. Take spoonfuls of the apple mixture and place them at intervals on the custard, like islands.

It is important to bake the apples, rather than stew them in the ordinary way, as this makes a stiffer purée which will keep its shape.

Many old apple recipes combined mixtures of meat, suet, spices and a proportion of apples, baked together in a pie. This is the origin of our modern mincemeat, after all, and one in which the apples give a wonderful moistness to the pie and also help to balance the fattiness of the meat. Sweet Lamb Pie is a traditional Cumbrian recipe, best made with meat from one of Beatrix Potter's beloved Herdwicks, the hardy, solid sheep which roam the Fells through the harshest weather, and whose meat has time to develop a wonderful flavour during the two years it takes this slow-growing breed to reach a weight at which they can be slaughtered. This is a recipe which might well have been made in the kitchen at Hill Top, Near Sawrey, Beatrix Potter's first farm in the Lake District, whose kitchen range figures in so many of the illustrations to her books, like *The Tale of the Pie and the Patty Pan*.

Sweet Lamb Pie

*8oz (225g) shortcrust
pastry
1lb (450g) shoulder of
lamb, trimmed of fat
and cut into small
cubes
salt and pepper
2oz (50g) soft brown
sugar*

*4oz (125g) currants
1 teaspoon (5ml) mixed
spice
2 large well-flavoured
eating apples, peeled,
cored and sliced
¼pt (150ml) unsweetened
apple juice*

Line a pie dish with half the pastry, put in a layer of the cubed lamb, season it with salt and pepper. Mix the brown sugar, currants and spice together and put a layer of this over the meat, then a layer of sliced apple. Continue until the ingredients have been used up, finishing with a layer of apple. Pour over enough apple juice to moisten but not drown the contents, roll out the remaining pastry and place it over the pie. Make slits in the top so that steam can escape, and decorate it with any trimmings. Bake in a moderate oven (350°F, 180°C; gas mark 4) for 50 minutes. This is as good cold as hot, as the apple keeps it moist.

Lengthy directions for storing fruit are given in most practical books of housewifery and range from storage in dry sand or ashes to straw. 'It is proper to gather Winter Apples without the Stalks, because they will soonest perish', stated the anonymous author of *Adam's Luxury & Eve's Cookery* in 1744, while the more modern books omit this useful piece of advice, but advise wrapping each apple in waxed paper. Pears need even more careful handling; judging the right time to pick them is crucial, since if too unripe, they will go gritty in storage, if too ripe, they will overripen to a woolly texture.

The following eighteenth-century recipe for stewed pears is one I use a great deal – it comes from Mrs Glasse's *The Art of Cookery* and needs little translation:

To Stew Pears

Pare six Pears, and either quarter them, or do them whole; but makes a pretty Dish with one whole, and the other cut in quarter, and the Cores taken out, lay them in a deep earthen Pot, with a few Cloves, a Piece of Lemon-peel, a Gill of Red Wine, and a quarter of a Pound of fine Sugar: If the Pears are very large, they will take half a Pound of Sugar, and half a Pint of Red Wine. Cover them close with brown Paper, and bake them till they are enough. Serve them hot or cold, just as you like them.

NB A gill is 5fl oz (125ml), and foil is a good substitute for brown paper. How long the pears take to cook depends very much on the variety of pear, but this recipe is best suited to hard cooking varieties in any case, so allow at least 3 hours in a low oven (300°F, 150°C; gas mark 2).

Rudyard Kipling is thought to have designed the elegant tunnel of pears and flowering climbing plants at Bateman's, the Jacobean house set in one of the most beautiful parts of Sussex, near Burwash, in which he lived until his death in 1936. The varieties from which the tunnel is composed include one called Winter Nelis – a pear that one Victorian book on orchards suggests that no garden should be without. Its slender growth makes it particularly suitable for training, on a wall or over an arch as here. It is a keeping pear, ripening in December, but lasting until January with care.

The pear now growing in Kipling's arch is Conference, a reliable old variety, and now the most widely grown pear in England. It is not known for a particularly fine flavour, which makes it a good cooking, rather than dessert, pear. This recipe is a favourite and is based on a recipe contemporary with Kipling's time at Bateman's, from a book called *The Gentle Art of Cookery*, by Mrs C.F. Leyel and Mrs Olga Hartley, first published in 1925.

Pear Croustades

1pt (500ml) dry cider
8oz (225g) sugar
1lb (450g) hard cooking
  pears

4 thick slices of stale
white bread
unsalted butter

Make a syrup by boiling the cider and sugar together for 10 minutes, allow this to cool a little and while it does so, peel, core and slice the pears. Poach them gently in the syrup until soft. Trim the slices of bread of their crusts and fry on both sides in the butter. Drain on kitchen paper and keep them warm in a low oven with the door ajar so that the bread remains crisp. Lift the pears, which should be just warm, from the syrup and arrange them on the croustades. Serve at once, with thick cream as an optional extra.

It is said that Sir Isaac Newton's favourite dish was baked quinces, which is somewhat perverse of him under the circumstances. My visit to his birthplace, Woolsthorpe Manor near Grantham in Lincolnshire, was a happy accident. The familiar National Trust sign to the house prompted a diversion to discover the modest stone manor house, set on the outskirts of the village of Colsterworth. In the garden is a large, gnarled apple tree, direct descendant of that which inspired Newton's discovery of the theory of gravity.

BAKED APPLE AND QUINCE DUMPLINGS

2 quinces
honey to taste
1oz (25g) butter

8oz (225g) sweet
shortcrust pastry
4 small cooking apples
1 egg, beaten

Peel and core the quinces, cut them into small pieces and stew them with a little water until soft. Add honey to sweeten them, remembering that the mixture has to act as a sweetener for the apples as well, and beat in the butter. Roll out the pastry and cut it into four. On each piece put a peeled and cored apple, then spoon the quince mixture into the cavities left by the cores. Draw up the pastry round each apple so that it is completely closed, pinching the edges together with dampened fingers. Trim off any surplus pastry and brush with beaten egg. Arrange on a baking sheet and bake in a hot oven (425°F, 220°C; gas mark 7) for 25–30 minutes. Brush with milk and sprinkle with sugar before serving, either hot or cold.

Quinces are often to be seen growing in National Trust gardens, or included in their orchards. Attingham Park, near Shrewsbury, produces fine quinces in a good year – they need plenty of sunshine and a good, deep moist soil – and Oxburgh Hall, near King's Lynn, has trees in the kitchen garden.

There are far more recipes for quinces than for pears in old cookery books, no doubt because quinces have to be cooked and cannot be eaten raw; 'raw quinces cause the Colick, Wind, and bad Digestion, therefore 'tis proper to boil them and sweeten them with Sugar.' Although beautiful – a rich gold – they are the most unpromising fruit at first sight because they are rock hard; this quality makes it all the more odd that they are not more widely available – their durability makes them better able to withstand the rough and tumble of marketing better than most fruit.

John Parkinson, writing of them in 1629, says: 'There is no fruit growing in this land that is of so many uses as this, serving as well to make many dishes of meat for the table as for banquets and much more for the Physicall vertues.' These virtues, as given by Gerard in his *Herball*, include the interesting idea that pregnant women who eat quinces will produce intelligent children, and, more reliably, that quinces, once cooked, are an excellent digestive. Quince jelly and quince paste both figure in old cookery books, and can be made by any suitable method for apple jelly, or by the method for fruit cheese on page 63; there are many old recipes for preserving them in syrup, which makes a very useful and instant dessert, or, drained of syrup and reheated with a little unsweetened apple juice, makes an excellent sauce to serve with roast pork instead of apple sauce, especially because of their digestive qualities.

The fruit of the Japanese quince, *chaenomeles*, can be substituted for quince, but it is usually better to use half japonica and half cooking apples (a very successful combination) because the former are so much smaller than quince and have huge cores.

To Preserve Quinces

Peel and quarter the quinces, and keep the peelings. Put the fruit into a pan, cover with water and spread the peelings over the surface to keep the fruit beneath the liquid. Cover the pan tightly and cook gently until the fruit is soft − it should also be a pretty pink by this time. Allow the fruit to cool. Fill Kilner jars with the fruit, then make enough syrup to top up the jars, in the proportion of 8oz (225g) sugar to 1pt (500ml) water, boiling it for 10–15 minutes until fairly thick. Pour this over the quinces, put the lids on the Kilner jars and put them in a large baking tin, on a wad of newspaper. Put in centre of the oven, set at 300°F, 150°C; gas mark 2 for $1\frac{1}{2}$–2 hours. Take out and screw on the metal bands. Leave until cold, then test to see that each jar is sealed. Any jar which has a defective seal can either be reprocessed in the oven with a fresh lid, or the contents can be frozen, although the texture of the fruit is not quite as good.

The orchard at Hardwick Hall has a number of interesting varieties of plums, gages and damsons, including a damson called Merryweather, which comes, like the Bramley apple, from the nearby town of Southwell. Plums and gages always seem praised at the expense of the damson, but while they make excellent eating raw, they are rarely as exciting cooked – even plum jam can be a little boring. Damsons, on the other hand, really come into their own once cooked; whether as puddings, jams, jellies or pickled, their fine, deep flavour is unsurpassed.

Some old damson trees have been pruned back into productivity in the garden of the Apprentice House at Styal by Mrs Brittan, who appreciates this traditional northern treat. They could be so prolific in a good year that, all over the village of Styal in the damson season, there would be the scent of the fruit being simmered into jams and jellies.

Bottled damsons can be ready at a moment's notice to translate into a pie, tart or crumble, but they can be particularly good on their own if the syrup is flavoured with rose-water, as recommended in many old recipes. Rose-scented geranium leaves can make as good an addition.

BOTTLED DAMSONS

Make a strong syrup (12oz [350g] sugar to each pint [500ml] of water), and add 2 geranium leaves to each pint as it simmers. Use this hot syrup to pour over the washed fruit in the Kilner jars, and proceed as for the previous recipe for preserved quinces.

Pickled damsons make one of the best accompaniments to cold ham or cold salt pork. There is an interesting eighteenth-century recipe 'To pickle Plumbs like Olives', which results in a very good, tart relish, especially when used with damsons.

PICKLED DAMSONS

Make a Pickle of white Wine Vinegar, Salt, Fennel Seed, and Dill; boil it with as much of these Ingredients, as will give the Pickle a perfect Taste of them. Then put in your Plumbs, and take them off the Fire soon after, let them stand till they are cold, then put them in Pots.

Alternatively, you can add sugar, at the rate of 12oz (350g) sugar to 1 pint (500ml) of wine or cider vinegar. Put all the ingredients in a pan and bring to the boil. Lift out the fruit into another bowl and let the vinegar syrup boil for another 5 minutes. Pour it over the fruit and leave overnight. Repeat the process twice more and you will have a fine, mellow pickle which will keep, if necessary, for years.

The following recipe is based on one which occurs in many a cookery book of the seventeenth century, for making the pastes that I mentioned at the start of the chapter. The method is substantially the same as that for making a fruit cheese, although sometimes a jelly method is used to obtain 'clear-cakes'. In some cases, as with certain types of plum, apple jelly was added to help the set.

To Make White Plum-paste

Take a Pound of fine Sugar, and a Pint of Water, or more, as the Quantity you intend to make requires; set it on the Fire, let it boil. Set a Pan of Water to boil, when it does, put in your Plums, as they slip their Skins off, take off the Skins and put the Plums into the Syrup. Boil them all to Pieces, and to a Quart of Plums put a Pint of Apple-Jelly; boil them well together, and rub it thro' a Hair Sieve. To a Pint of this put a Pound and a half of sifted Sugar, let the Jelly boil before you shake the Sugar, and let it scald till the Sugar is well melted; skin it, put it in Pots, and dry it in the Stove.

A Modern Fruit Cheese

6lb (2.70kg) fruit (plums
or damsons, or a
mixture)

1pt (500ml) water
5lb (2kg) sugar

Wash the fruit, remove any stalks or blemishes, wasp holes and so on, then halve and remove the stones. Put all into a large casserole and add the water. Bake in a low oven (275°F, 140°C; gas mark 1) until the fruit is pulpy, then leave to cool. Push the fruit through a coarse sieve or food mill. Weigh the fruit pulp and put it into a heavy pan, adding a pound of sugar to each pound of pulp. Bring slowly to the boil, stirring often, then simmer steadily for about $1\frac{1}{4}$ hours, scraping the bottom of the pan from time to time. When the mixture begins to candy (ie look sugary rather than syrupy), it is ready. Pout it into shallow dishes – foil pie plates are ideal, if not very historical – lightly oiled with almond oil, and leave in a warm place covered with greaseproof paper for a day or so, until the cheese has shrunk and dried a little. Remove the paper and allow to become quite cold, before covering with fresh paper and wrapping the whole thing in cling-film. Store in a cool, dry place and they will keep for at least two years, improving all the time. The cheeses can either be cut into thin slices, rolled in sugar and served as sweetmeats, or eaten as an accompaniment to cold meats (particularly good with cold ham, or smoked chicken). You can also turn them on to a shallow dish, stick them with blanched and split almonds and surround with cream, as a dessert. The same method will do for quinces.

Mulberries are also to be found in many Trust gardens, some old, some newly planted; the oldest are to be found at Clevedon Court, near Bristol, and at Charlecote Park in Warwickshire, while they have been freshly planted at Wightwick Manor near Wolverhampton. Canons Ashby has a tree which yields enough fruit every year for mulberry pie to be made and served to visitors, who rarely fail to succumb to the atmosphere of this magic place, especially when eating mulberry pie. Hardwick has a fine mulberry walk, and the tree at Upton House provided light refreshment on the warm afternoon in late summer when I visited it, rather to the surprise of one or two other visitors who thought that the squashy black fruit we were eating from the grass beneath the tree must be poisonous.

Mulberries should not be picked, as they only develop their full, unique flavour (that of a sun-warmed raspberry crossed with a very ripe, sweet blackberry) when they actually drop off the tree. The black mulberry (*Morus nigra*) is the one to plant in the garden for fruit; the white mulberry has insignificant fruit without much flavour, but is the one whose leaves are beloved by silk-worms. Richard Bradley also noted that the black mulberry rarely made 'a strait Stem of any good Height', and advised grafting it on to 'Stocks of the White Mulberry, which naturally grows strait, and will make a handsome Tree very quickly'. I have just planted a black mulberry in my garden, and so far Bradley has been proved right – it is already showing signs of being anything but straight.

I feel that the very best way to enjoy mulberries is to treat them like raspberries, only cooking them if really necessary. They are delicious as part of a summer pudding and especially good eaten with a little honey and lots of Greek yoghurt, which is how I have enjoyed them in Greece. However, if you want to prolong the pleasure of any that you have, the following recipe should do it.

CLEAR MULBERRY AND APPLE JELLY

equal quantities of   *water to cover*
 mulberries and apples   *sugar*

Remove any blemishes from the apples, then cut them up roughly and put them in the pan with the mulberries. Add just enough water to come level with the top of the fruit. Heat the fruit slowly, then simmer fast until the apples are soft. Tip into a jelly bag, or an old clean pillowcase, and leave to drip overnight into a large bowl. Next day, measure the juice and return it to the preserving pan with 1lb of sugar (450g) to each pint (500ml) juice. Stir over a medium heat until the sugar has dissolved, then boil fast to setting point.

Medlar trees are very attractive as part of a mixed orchard; small and sometimes almost squat, they have enormous character. The fruit has an odd flavour, 'rather like cold apple purée' as the gardener who sold me my tree told me, achieved by picking the unripe fruit and leaving it to ripen, or blet, until almost rotten. The flowers are obviously attractive – large and white, balanced delicately among the big crinkled leaves – but I first appreciated the beauty of the fruit when I saw the tree which grows at Standen, that comfortable Victorian house in West Sussex designed by Philip Webb and decorated and furnished by his friend and colleague William Morris. The medlar is a fruit of distinctly Pre-Raphaelite appearance, and well worth growing for that alone; they can be seen in many gardens of the National Trust, including those at Westbury Court and Moseley Old Hall. I have never had enough medlars to try the following recipe, but I include it for the interest of anyone who has.

To Make a Tart of Medlers

Take Medlers that be rotten, and stamp them, and set them upon a chaffin dish with coales, and beat in two yolks of Eggs, boyling till it be somewhat thick, then season it with Sugar, Cinamon, and Ginger, and lay it in paste.

In other words, thicken a purée of medlars with egg yolk and heat it gently (I disagree with the author of the recipe here – if you boil it, it will be medlar-flavoured scrambled egg) until it thickens. Sugar it to taste, and add the spices, again to taste. Put it into a prepared flan case and bake.

Walnut are most often planted as specimen trees, rather than as part of an orchard. Wimpole Hall, near Cambridge, has a fine collection, some taken from the garden of St John's Jerusalem, near Dartford in Kent, which was badly damaged in the severe storm of 1987. It is not an indigenous tree, as its name indicates: the prefix 'wal' denotes it as a foreigner, introduced into this country in the fifteenth century. Most recipes given are for pickling green walnuts, which is a pity, since nothing is better than a fresh, ripe walnut, harvested from the ground when they drop in September. They ripen perfectly well in this country, as I found even when living in Cumberland, so it is worth planting a tree if you have space. While waiting the long ten years or so before any nuts appear, the aromatic leaves can be made into an infusion and used as a rinse for dark hair, and bunched and hung in wardrobes to repel moths.

This tip for 'reviving' walnuts comes from an Edwardian book. It certainly works wonders for the stale nuts sold just before Christmas.

To Revive Walnuts

Dry old walnuts should be soaked in cold milk some hours in their brown shells, *unopened*, and when you crack them you will find the nuts have swelled and fill the inside of the walnut shells, they peel easily, and are mellowed generally.

This recipe for walnut pie is something of a curiosity, but it makes a dish which accompanies a rich beef casserole remarkably well, and will obligingly bake in the oven and thus make the perfect vegetable dish. You can use the packet nuts sold for baking, but it is much better made with freshly cracked nuts. It is another interesting item from *The Gentle Art of Cookery*.

Walnut Pie

Put a thick layer of mashed potato in a buttered pie dish and season with salt, pepper and a little nutmeg. Chop finely enough walnuts to cover the potatoes. Make half a pint of good gravy from beef stock (or a cube), thickened with a little cornflour and seasoned with a spoonfull or two of mushroom ketchup. Cover with another layer of seasoned mashed potato, dot with butter, and bake until brown and crunchy on top.

Richard Bradley suggested, in his directions for orchards with which I began the chapter, hedging them with 'Filberds and Barberries'. There are many Trust gardens which have fine displays of the former – Sissinghurst has its Nuttery, there is a Nut Walk at Moseley Old Hall, and at Upton the Nut Alley is being restored – but I have failed to find any Barberries. The decorative slim oval bright red berries of *Berberis vulgaris* (now a rare shrub) were much used in cookery, both to garnish dishes, and to make a tart jam or jelly, rather in the way we still use rowan berries. I have a feeling it won't be too long before an enterprising Trust gardener takes up the challenge and fulfils Bradley's instructions to the letter.

The Fruit Garden

THE FRUIT GARDEN

ERHAPS the pleasantest kitchen gardens are those where fruit, vegetables, herbs and flowers grow in disciplined abundance, the kind of planting that Thomas Tusser advocates in his bouncy doggerel work *Five Hundred Points of Good Husbandry*, in 1573:

> The gooseberry, respis, and roses all three,
> With strawberries beneath them, do trimly agree.

The gardens where this planting is carried out on purpose, rather than on the haphazard method of planting anything wherever there is room, are called by the French word *potagers*, since that is where the style originated. This could be due to the French admiration for anything edible, but it produces a garden far more beautiful and elegantly productive than the more rigid segregation of the typical Victorian or Edwardian kitchen garden, although these have their charms. Gardens like that at Villandry, on the banks of the Loire near Tours, combine the formality of standard roses and free-standing fruit trees trained into club-like shapes with vegetables grown in box-edged beds intersected by gravel paths. A rather softer and more relaxed *potager* can be seen at West Green House.

I first saw this wonderful garden in August, a time of year when such gardens are at their most opulent, and becoming just a little overblown. Here the beds of vegetables, herbs and fruit ray out like the spokes of a wheel from the hubs, which are in the form of ornamental fruit cages. Gooseberry bushes are grown as standards, a much more convenient height for picking the fruit, as well as being very decorative. This technique has the added advantage of providing extra space round the feet of the bushes, very useful for those whose fruit growing is curbed by lack of room.

Another charming *potager*, smaller and even more informal than that at West Green, is at Tintinhull in Somerset. Here currants, raspberries and strawberries share a small part of this exquisite garden, jostling for position with nepeta and roses, with alpine strawberries forming a productive and decorative edging in some places.

Mrs Raffald's recipe for Raspberry Brandy is most evocative of such gardens:

> Gather the raspberries when the sun is hot upon them, and as soon as ever you have got them, to every five quarts of raspberries put one quart of the best brandy, boil a quart of water five minutes with a pound of double-refined sugar in it, and pour it boiling hot on the berries, let it stand all night, then add nine quarts more brandy, stir it about very well, put it in a stone bottle, and let it stand a month or six weeks; when fine, bottle it.

My own recipe, which I make every year, is rather more modest in the amount of brandy required:

RASPBERRY BRANDY

12oz (350g) freshly picked raspberries	*1pt (500ml) good, but not best, brandy*
	6oz (175g) caster sugar

Put the raspberries in a large jar, mashing them a little with a wooden spoon, then pour the brandy over. Cover tightly and leave for 48 hours. Strain through a muslin-lined sieve, then add the sugar, stirring until it has completely dissolved. Return to the jar, cover again and leave for a month or so, as Mrs Raffald suggests, to allow any sediment to sink to the bottom, then bottle, cork tightly and leave another 3 months before drinking. For a slightly weaker drink, follow Mrs Raffald's method and pour $\frac{1}{4}$ pint (150ml) boiling water mixed with 1oz (25g) of the sugar over the raspberries. Add $\frac{1}{4}$ pint (150ml) of the brandy and leave as above, strain and add the remaining brandy and the sugar.

This is not only very good as an after-dinner liqueur, but as an addition to a winter fruit salad, or to sauces both sweet and savoury — try a raspberry brandy sauce with duck, for instance.

Another very traditional English product of the fruit garden, raspberry vinegar, makes one of the most refreshing long drinks, topped up with cold mineral water, either still or carbonated.

Raspberry Vinegar

1lb (450g) raspberries	*6oz (175g) sugar to each*
1pt (500ml) white wine	*pint*
or cider vinegar	

Crush the raspberries and add to the vinegar in a large jar, cover, and leave in a cool place for a fortnight, stirring from time to time. Strain through muslin into a jug, measure the liquid, which will be rather more than the original pint, and add sugar accordingly. Put in a heavy pan, stir until boiling, then boil for ten minutes. Leave to cool, then bottle.

NB Other fruit vinegars can be made the same way.

In the newly emerging kitchen garden at Calke Abbey, old varieties of soft fruit are being grown, including the Yellow Antwerp raspberry recommended by J. C. Loudon in the middle of the last century. This is essentially a dessert raspberry, unsuitable for jam or jelly though very sweet and delicious, but, as with all yellow raspberries, lacking that sharp delicacy of flavour.

The following recipe is a useful one; I began to make it every summer when we had red, white and black currants all producing fruit simultaneously, but it works equally well with red and yellow raspberries. It doesn't have a very romantic name, but it might be rechristened Toxopholite Tart, in memory of those Edwardian ladies who passed time in practising their archery.

Target Tart

pastry cream (see p.102)	*4–6oz (125–175g)*
1 baked pâte sucrée flan	*yellow raspberries*
case (see p.101)	*(or substitute white*
12oz (350g) red	*currants)*
raspberries	*sugar to taste*

Spread the pastry cream over the base of the flan case, then arrange the berries in concentric circles; aim at having red in the centre and again around the edge. Sprinkle with sugar to taste. If you are using red, white and black currants, cook each colour separately with a very little water and sugar to taste, just long enough to soften the fruit, and arrange with black in the centre and red around the outside.

Calke's 'antique' currants include varieties such as Goliath, Fays Prolific and White Dutch. These days, more black currants are grown than either red or white, but for hundreds of years black currants lacked popularity. John Parkinson gives brief and accurate details of the gastronomic uses of the various kinds in his *Garden of Pleasant Flowers* (1629):

> The red Currans are usually eaten when they are ripe, as a refreshing to an hot stomacke in the heate of the yeare, which by the tartnesse is much delighted. Some preserve them, and conserve them also as other fruits, and spend them at neede. The white Currans, by reason of the more pleasant winie taste, are more accepted and desired, as also because they are more daintie, and lesse common. Some use both the leaves and berries of the blacke Curran in sawces and other meates, and are well pleased both with the flower and taste thereof, although many mislike it.

Richard Bradley, writing a hundred years later, said that all three kinds of currants should be planted, including 'the Kind which bears the Black Fruit, for Variety sake, as well as on account of its great Virtue in Medicine, should not be wanting in a Garden, tho' scarce one in twenty can like its flavour'.

Here is a very medicinal recipe for a Blackcurrant Rob, the reduced juice of the fruit entirely without additives, not even water. It is worth trying if you have enough fruit; it makes a delicious winter drink for a cold, topped up with hot water and honey, or as an addition to fruit salads. The eighteenth-century method of preserving it is not very reliable, and as it contains no sugar it is best to freeze it in ice-trays and take out a lump when required.

BLACKCURRANT ROB

Pick blackcurrants when perfectly ripe, strig them, then put them in a covered casserole in a low to moderate oven (350°F, 180°C; gas mark 4) for about two hours, or until the juice has started to run from the fruit. Tip them into a strong pillowcase and twist the ends tightly, then wring the bundle over a large pan to extract the juice. Simmer the juice over a low heat until it thickens and looks syrupy, then cool and freeze in ice-trays. Store the frozen cubes in a plastic bag.

One of the best strawberry jam recipes I have ever tasted is the following from *A New System of Domestic Cookery* (1818 edition); it is more of a preserve than a jam, too good for bread and butter but wonderful for serving, as the author suggests, with thin cream (or with *fromage frais*), as a dessert. It uses red currant juice instead of water and is therefore very useful if you have a prolific crop of red currants but few strawberries.

To Preserve Strawberries Whole

Take equal weights of the fruit and double-refined sugar; lay the former in a large dish, and sprinkle half the sugar in fine powder, over; give a gentle shake to the dish, that the sugar may touch the under side of the fruit. Next day make a thin syrup [see below] with the remainder of the sugar, and, instead of water, allow one pint of red-currant juice to every pound of strawberries; in this simmer them until sufficiently jellied. Choose the largest scarlets, or others, when not dead-ripe. In either of the above ways, they eat well served in thin cream, in glasses.

This recipe needs no translation, except to say that I use ordinary granulated sugar for it. Make the syrup by strigging the currants and just covering them with water. Simmer slowly until the fruit is very soft (if you can do this in the oven, the flavour will be even better). Tip the fruit into a jelly bag and allow to drip overnight into the pan with the rest of the juice.

The recipe works very well with other fruit, and I have found it particularly effective when a white currant syrup is used for alpine strawberries – such as those at Tintinhull – in a good year when I have enough to fill half a dozen small jars.

A really fine-flavoured strawberry, such as the Royal Sovereign variety being grown at Calke, is best kept for something even more special:

To Preserve Strawberries in Wine

Put a quantity of the finest large strawberries into a gooseberry bottle, and strew in three large spoonfuls of fine sugar; fill up with Madeira wine, or fine sherry.

Use a large Kilner or other preserving jar, and keep the finished product in a cool dark place. It is lovely to bring out at Christmas, as it has all the scent of summer.

At Polesden Lacey in Surrey, Mrs Ronnie Greville held her famous weekend house parties from the beginning of the century to the outbreak of the Second World War. Her guests included literary figures, prominent politicians, Russian princes and Indian maharajahs, and in 1923 she lent Polesden to the future George VI and Queen Elizabeth for part of their honeymoon. Her menu books still survive, and the produce of what must have been an extensive kitchen garden figures largely. Mrs Greville insisted on strawberries almost the year round, which appear frequently in the menus. Although the kitchen garden no longer exists, the spirit of that era is very much alive, nowhere more strongly than in the collection of photographs in the Smoking Room. The following recipe is very typical of the style of cooking at Polesden, French in origin but not particularly elaborate, a recipe from one of the books in which X. Marcel Boulestin introduced French cooking to English palates during the 1920s and '30s.

FRAISES PRALINÉES

Take a pound of strawberries, cut them in two, or, if very large, in four. Also take two oranges, remove very carefully with a really sharp knife skin and pith, and cut them in thin quarters. Do this over a cup so that the juice which is bound to come out is not wasted, put together in a bowl oranges and strawberries, the juice of the oranges, soft sugar, a glassful of dry white wine, and a liqueur-glassful of brandy. Shake well and put on ice for a little while. Sprinkle with chopped grilled almonds and serve very cold.

No chapter on soft fruit is complete without a recipe for Summer Pudding. This recipe comes from Christine Milson, who serves this in the restaurant at Beningbrough Hall, near York.

SUMMER PUDDING

6 slices stale white bread   *4oz (125g) sugar*
1½lb (675g) mixed summer
* fruit – strawberries,*
* raspberries, blackcurrants,*
* cherries, blackberries*

Remove the crusts from the bread and cut into neat fingers. Use some of these to line a 2 pint (1.25l) pudding basin. Cook the fruit with the sugar and 5 tablespoons (75ml) water until the juice runs from it, then put half the mixture into the basin. Cover with some of the bread, add the rest of the mixture and use the last of the bread to form a lid. Put a small plate on top and a heavy weight on top of that. Leave to refrigerate overnight. Next day, turn the pudding out and decorate with fresh fruit.

NB Summer pudding can be made really special by using slices of sponge cake to line the basin instead of bread.

Of course, it wasn't only the large houses and their extensive kitchen gardens which produced quantities of soft fruit. In west Surrey, the National Trust owns picturesque Oakhurst Cottage, painted with such devastating charm by Helen Allingham, the Edwardian watercolour artist who did much to popularise the English rural scene. It is a cottage which has remained untouched by the sort of gentrification which usually robs such sixteenth-century buildings of their character; the Trust has preserved it as a nineteenth-century labourer's dwelling, and the garden is an appropriate mixture of beans, onions, cabbages, hollyhocks and roses, gooseberry and currant bushes.

GOOSEBERRY AND BLACK CURRANT JAM

Take equal weight of pounded lump-sugar and picked fruit; strew the sugar over the fruit in the preserving-pan, and put a little water into it. Let it soak; then boil and skim it; lift a little of the juice and fruit when the fruit has boiled for about twelve minutes and set it to cool on a plate. If the juice runs off, the jam must be boiled longer; if it jellies, though slightly, it is enough.

Gooseberries and Elderflowers

The combination of the tartness of gooseberries and fragrant elderflowers is one which has stood the test of time. Gooseberry wine flavoured thus was called English 'Frontignan' after the wine made with muscatel grapes, the flavour of which it resembles if not rivals. Try poaching the first, green, gooseberries of the season with a little water, a moderate amount of sugar, and two heads of elderflowers per pound of fruit. A gooseberry fool, flavoured in the same way, is very good, and the following sorbet is pure magic.

Gooseberry Sorbet

1lb (450g) gooseberries, topped and tailed	*2oz (50g) caster sugar*
	2–3 heads elderflowers
½pt (250ml) water	*2 egg whites*

Put the gooseberries, water, sugar and flowers (don't wash these if you can help it, but give each head a good shake to get rid of any insects) into a covered dish and put them to cook in a slow oven (300°F, 150°C; gas mark 2) for an hour or until soft. Remove the elderflowers and strain the fruit from the syrup, which should be reserved. Purée the fruit, preferably through the medium screen on a food mill to get rid of most of the pips. Stir in the remaining syrup gradually, stopping when you have a thick soup. Check for sweetness, adding more sugar if necessary, or a little lemon juice. Put this in a shallow plastic box with a lid and freeze until frozen round the edges but still soft in the centre – about 3 hours. Tip into a chilled bowl and beat with chilled beaters until smooth. Return to the fridge while you whisk the egg whites until stiff, then fold them into the gooseberry purée. Return to the freezer and freeze until required. Put the sorbet in the fridge for about ½ hour to thaw a little before serving.

Gooseberries flourish in cool, damp climates so I was not surprised to find that at East Riddlesden Hall, on the outskirts of Keighley in West Yorkshire, they had been planted in the garden there. This seventeenth-century manor house sits comfortably, together with its splendid barn and ancient fishpond, for all the world as if it were still surrounded by rolling fields and open country instead of the sprawl of an industrial town. The garden has recently been planted with herbs on the south-eastern side, and with a small orchard of apples and pears. Old northern varieties of gooseberries and currants flourish, alongside an important herb used as a sweetener whenever sugar was scarce. Called Sweet Cicely (*Myrrhis odorata*), the ferny leaves added to tart fruit remove the acidity without adding a cloying sweetness; eaten raw, the leaves have an aniseed flavour, but this disappears with cooking. The herb grows wild in the north of England, and should be planted with care in the garden as it can quickly colonise more than its allotted space. Mint, another herb not daunted by a cold climate, is also traditionally eaten with gooseberries in the north. The following recipe is for a raised gooseberry pie, using the same type of hot-water crust as for pork pies, only sweetened. The gooseberries make a wonderful contrast with the richness of the pastry, and it is excellent cold.

RAISED GOOSEBERRY PIE

Pastry

1lb (450g) plain flour
pinch of salt
1oz (25g) icing sugar

7fl oz (200ml) water
6oz (175g) lard

Filling

1–1½lb (450–675g)
  gooseberries
3oz (75g) sugar
2 tablespoons (30ml)
  fresh sweet cicely
  (if unavailable, use
  extra sugar), chopped

1 teaspoon (5ml) fresh
  mint, chopped
¼pt (150ml) apple jelly
  (see p.54)

To make the pastry, sift the flour, salt and icing sugar into a bowl and make a hollow in the middle. Put the water and lard into a small saucepan, warm until the lard has melted, then raise the heat and, when the mixture is boiling, pour it on to the flour. Stir rapidly with a wooden spoon until all the flour is incorporated, knead the pastry briefly and form it into a ball. Leave, covered with a teacloth, until cool enough to roll out.

In the meantime, select something around which to mould the pastry – a large Kilner jar is fine – make sure it is quite clean and dry, then flour it so that the pastry will slip off it easily. When the pastry has cooled but is still warm and malleable, roll out two-thirds to about ½in (1.25cm) thick, and fit it around the Kilner jar, trimming off any extra. Leave for about 5 minutes, then ease the jar out. Fill this crust with the topped and tailed gooseberries mixed with the sugar and chopped herbs. Roll out the remaining pastry and use to make a lid, decorate with pastry leaves, and make a small round hole in the centre. Roll up a small tube of cardboard or stiff paper and put it in the hole. Transfer the pie to a baking sheet and bake the pie at 375°F, 190°C; gas mark 5 for about 1 hour, or until the pastry is a rich golden brown. About 15 minutes before the pie is ready, sprinkle the top with sugar. Remove from the oven and take out the cardboard tube; if serving warm, then leave for about half an hour before serving with cream or custard. If serving cold, warm the apple jelly until just melted and pour it in through the hole in the lid, then leave to cool completely.

In simple cottage gardens, where rhubarb grows unchecked, it might be forced by covering it with anything that comes to hand – old buckets, discarded coal scuttles, even worn-out coal hods. In elegant kitchen gardens, rhubarb forcing pots add considerably to the scene. When visiting Trust gardens for this book, I grew used to the sight of tall slim terracotta pots, each with its burgeoning tuft of rhubarb leaves bursting through the top where the forcing lids had been removed. They can be seen at Barrington Court, West Green House and Felbrigg and very elegant they look, much better than old buckets. Both at Calke Abbey and in the garden of the Apprentice House at Styal, local varieties of rhubarb are being grown – Timperley Early, for instance, originated in what is now a suburb of Manchester only a few miles north of Styal.

The first rhubarb sent to England in the middle of the eighteenth century was grown at the Botanical Gardens in Edinburgh, but the 3rd Earl of Egremont was amongst the earliest cultivators of it as a garden plant, at Petworth. It took another hundred years to become established as the carefully nurtured plant of Victorian and Edwardian gardeners. It was appreciated for its health-giving properties as well as its delicate flavour when forced, and so stewed rhubarb became a stalwart of the nursery and schoolroom, particularly when accompanied by custard.

RHUBARB COMPÔTE

The delicate pink of forced rhubarb makes a wonderful *compôte*, cooked very gently indeed in orange juice and sweetened with honey, then served very cold with sweet biscuits. The bright orange and pink colour combination makes it quite exotic enough to serve at a dinner party.

Rhubarb pie can also be very good, particularly when the pastry lid is 'finished' with a kind of meringue topping made in the Edwardian fashion.

EDWARDIAN FRUIT PIES

Make a fruit pie according to your usual recipe, and about 15 minutes before it is ready to leave the oven reduce the heat, if necessary, to about 350°F, 180°C; gas mark 4. Whisk 4 tablespoons (60ml) caster sugar and 1 egg white together until stiff and spread this over the pie crust with a fork, roughing the surface into peaks. Return to the oven until this meringue has set and the peaks have browned a little.

But the aristocrats of the fruit garden are the wall-trained fruit – the peaches, apricots and cherries. Morello cherries, which make such delicious jam, will obligingly occupy a north wall, leaving the warmer walls to the peaches and apricots which need them. Fan-trained cherries can be seen at Nunnington Hall, where they serve another good tart made from their own morellos. Mr Squires, the gardener in charge at Nunnington, told me that the fruit should always be cut from the tree, as disease can enter through the wounds made by pulling it off. Canons Ashby has wall-trained cherries in the Green Court, and Ham House at Richmond in Surrey has a number in the Cherry Garden to the east of the house. Seventeenth-century recipes contemporaneous with Ham House call for cherries to be cooked with plenty of spice – one recipe adds mustard to a cherry pie. Black cherries are certainly good if spiced according to the recipe for spiced peaches on p.82, and they should be used for the following recipes.

SUGARED CHERRIES

3lb (1.35kg) ripe but firm black cherries, with their stalks on if possible

3lb (1.35kg) sugar
1½pt (750ml) water

Trim the cherry stalks to 1in (2.5cm). Make a syrup of the sugar and water and add the fruit. Simmer slowly until the cherries begin to look transparent, rather like *glacé* cherries. Drain the fruit from the syrup and spread it out on cake racks. Leave overnight in a warm dry place. Next day spread them out on greaseproof paper and leave in an airing cupboard for another 24 hours. Pack into a plastic box, layering them with waxed paper. To serve as sweets, dust them with icing sugar first, or dip each into a little melted plain chocolate.

To Make Cherry Brandy

Take black Cherries, when they are at the cheapest, and pulling them from the Stalks, put them into a Cask of Brandy, a Pound to each Quart of Brandy, and one Pound of fine Sugar to each Gallon. Let it stand for some time, and draw it off. It will be very rich.

An excellent seventeenth-century recipe which needs no adapting, the proportions are: 1lb (450g) cherries, 2 pints (1.25l) brandy, 2oz (50g) sugar. The fruit can be used to add to fruit salads, to make ice-cream, and to add to pies.

The German influence in Victorian cooking meant that cherries began to make an appearance with meat dishes, which was, and still is, popular in Germany. The following is Francatelli's quick cherry sauce to serve with venison and hare, and was a recipe which probably found favour with Prince Albert.

Cherry Sauce

Put a pot of black currant jelly into a stewpan, together with six ounces of dried cherries, a small stick of cinnamon, and a dozen cloves tied up in a piece of muslin; moisten with half a pint of red wine, and set the whole to simmer gently on a slow fire for ten minutes; then take out the cinnamon and cloves and send to table.

NB Dried cherries seem to have been the same as sugared cherries (see previous recipe), judging by the instructions on how to dry them – *glacé* cherries would be far too sweet, so if no sugared cherries are available, use fresh, tinned or brandied cherries in preference.

Many of the walls of old kitchen gardens served a dual purpose, being built as hot walls, with flues at intervals so that the heat generated would ripen peaches and apricots and protect the blossom from late frosts. It is still sometimes possible to see the skeletal remains of framework which supported blinds made of oiled paper or of hessian, that could be rolled down to protect fruit or blossom. Such walls and remains can be seen in the delightful walled garden at Greys Court, with a more complete version of the system at Westbury Court. Here the Trust has been working to restore a garden created during the reign of William III, including the introduction of pre-1700 plants and fruit trees. At Sizergh Castle in Cumbria, a hot wall supports a Brown Turkey fig tree.

However successful these methods might have been in helping to ripen fruit, many recipes are given in old cookery books for unripe fruit. This was partly because it was necessary to remove some before the fruit matured in order to produce finer specimens, but also, I suspect, because of Britain's uncertain climate.

To Preserve Green Peaches

In some Gardens, where the Trees are pruned and ordered, by a skilful hand, it is often that a Tree will be so full of Fruit, that it is necessary to take away some, when they are green, that the others may swell the better ...

Scald your green Peaches in Water, then, with a Cloth, rub the Down from them; then put them, in more Water, over a slow Fire, and let them stew till they are green, keeping them cover'd. Then take their weight in fine Sugar, and with some Water, boil it to a Syrup, taking off the Scum as it rises; then put in your Peaches, and boil them till they are clear and put them, with the Syrup, in Glasses, or Gally-pots; and when they are cold, cover them with Paper. Note, You must gather your Peaches before the Stone is hard in them, which you may know by putting a Pin through them.

From the same book (Richard Bradley's *The Country Lady's Director*) comes the following recipe for peach jam which needs little translation. Peel the peaches by dipping in boiling water.

Marmalade of Peaches

Take Peaches, well grown and almost ripe; pare them, and take their Flesh clean from the Stones. Lay them with a little Water into a Stew-Pan, and add three Quarters of their weight of fine Sugar powder'd. Let this stew till the Peaches are tender, and then mash them with a Spoon, letting them boil gently all the while, till the Whole becomes thick.

Mr Bradley suggests that this jam makes very good jam tarts, but he uses the rather lugubrious eighteenth-century term for a pastry case, calling it a 'Coffin':

Make some Coffins of sweet Paste, and when they are gently baked, and cold, fill them with the above-mentioned Marmalade of Peaches and serve them.

More elaborate peach desserts appear in Victorian and Edwardian cookery books – a period when food became exceedingly formal. I have adapted the following recipe from a famous Victorian Scottish cookery book, *The Cook and Housewife's Manual*, by Mistress Margaret Dods. It is both good and economical – peaches are 'stretched' by the addition of an apple purée:

MISTRESS DODS' DRESSED PEACHES

5oz (150g) sugar
½pt (250ml) water
4 'very fine' peaches

2lb (900g) Bramley
apples
lemon juice
ratafia biscuits

Make a syrup by melting the sugar in the water and bringing it to the boil. Simmer for 10 minutes. Add the peaches and let them simmer in the syrup for another 7 minutes. Take the pan off the heat and leave the peaches to soak in the syrup while you prepare the apple purée. Peel, core and slice the apples and put them in a pan with a couple of spoonfuls of the syrup in which the peaches are soaking. Cook slowly with a lid on the pan until the apples are soft, then beat them to a snow with a wooden spoon, adding more sugar if necessary. Put a layer of this purée in a glass bowl. Slip the skins off the peaches, halve them and remove the stones, then cut them into eighths. Arrange these slices on the apple purée, then cover with the remaining purée. Boil down the remaining syrup until thick, add lemon juice to sharpen the flavour, and pour over the fruit. Decorate with ratafias.

Pickled peaches are always popular and make an excellent Christmas present. There are many recipes for them, and one suggests stuffing the pickled peaches with mixtures of mustard and garlic, or with horseradish and ginger. This is not as outlandish as it sounds – a pickled peach, halved and spread with a coarse-grain mustard and sprinkled with a little brown sugar, then slipped under the grill until the sugar bubbles, makes a delicious accompaniment to hot ham dishes.

PICKLED PEACHES

ripe peaches
white wine vinegar
golden caster sugar

whole cloves, allspice
berries and cinnamon
sticks

Dip each peach briefly in boiling water and slip off the skin. Pack them into clean Kilner jars. Measure the amount of liquid required (fill each jar with water to cover the peaches, then tip the water back into a measuring jug), and make a spiced syrup in the following proportion: to each pint (500ml) of wine vinegar add 1lb (450g) golden caster sugar and ½ oz (12g) of each of the spices, tied in a piece of muslin. Simmer this syrup for 20 minutes, then pour hot over the peaches in their jars. Seal at once and store in a cool dark place for at least 2 months before eating.

Apricots are another delectable wall-fruit, best eaten warm from the tree if one is lucky. Mrs Beeton gives a recipe for poaching green apricots (see green peaches on p.81) in a syrup, and ripe apricots gently simmered in a syrup flavoured with a vanilla pod and served very cold are delicious; the vanilla will even add flavour to weary shop fruit. But the following recipe, which is another of Mrs Leyel's, is simplicity itself; it rises spectacularly and is the most ethereal of soufflés.

APRICOT SOUFFLÉS

1lb (450g) ripe apricots	*3 egg whites*
1 teaspoon (5ml) Kirsch	*4 tablespoons (60ml)*
or other fruit eau-de-vie	*vanilla sugar*

Halve the apricots and remove the stones, then put the fruit into a blender or food processor and reduce to a purée. Stir in the Kirsch. Whip the egg whites until stiff, folding in the sugar half way through. Fold into the apricot purée and spoon into 4–6 individual soufflé dishes. Bake until well risen (about 15 minutes) at 375°F, 190°C; gas mark 5. Serve at once with a jug of thin chilled cream.

Not all National Trust gardens are museums of old varieties of fruit. At Beningbrough Hall, I was impressed to find that kiwi fruit are being grown as wall fruit. Mr Walker, the Head Gardener, points out proudly that they produce plenty of 'very tasty fruit', grown outside on south-, east- and west-facing walls. Best picked in October, they can be knocked back by a hard frost, but recover quickly. Although the kiwi fruit first began making its appearance in this country just before the last war (when it was still known as the Chinese Gooseberry, now a name given to the carambola), it is only in the last few years that it has really become readily available and reasonably cheap. It has also been somewhat abused, partly because of its all-too-amiable quality of looking fresh and tempting long after most other fruit have begun to reveal their age. It is quite surprisingly acid and so reacts badly with gelatine, and with cream, but it is worth including in one's diet as a very pleasant way to absorb a large amount of vitamin C.

The following recipe is based on one served in the tea-room at Powis Castle, and given to me by Mrs Henry, who uses strawberries but suggests using other fruit as well. Kiwi fruit combine well with the local Welsh goats' cheese which she uses:

Kiwi Salad with Goats' Cheese
For each serving

1 plain soft goats' cheese	*vinaigrette made with*
shredded iceberg lettuce	*tarragon vinegar and*
1 kiwi fruit	*sunflower oil*
	chopped walnuts

Arrange the cheese on a bed of shredded lettuce and arrange the peeled and sliced kiwi fruit around it. Spoon the vinaigrette over and garnish with the walnuts. Serve with warm crusty brown rolls as a first course.

Finally, a fitting tribute to the great horticulturalist J. C. Loudon – a mixed fruit brandy, the recipe for which I found in Margaret Dods' *The Cook and Housewife's Manual*. It calls for greengages and magnums (magnum bonum plums, dating from the sixteenth century), both of which grow as wall-fruit at Westbury Court. Alternatives can be found, although with a lessening of flavour.

Loudon's Admirable

Skin two dozen ripe peaches. Quarter them and take out the stones. Add to this the pulp of two dozen ripe greengages, and of one dozen ripe magnums. For every four pounds of pulp add six of sugar and two quarts of water. Boil slowly for a half-hour or more. Skim, strain, and, when cool, add three quarts of brandy or flavourless whisky.

The Orangery and Hothouse

The Orangery and Hothouse

T is striking to note how many recipes there are for dishes using oranges and lemons in old cookery books, when their high price (six silver pence for a lemon at a feast given for Henry VIII and Anne Boleyn by one of the livery companies) must have put them out of the reach of many a cook. By the end of the eighteenth century, they had become the most easily grown 'exotic' fruit, with elegant buildings to house the tender trees gracing many a garden of grand country houses; this meant, however, that they remained in the luxury class until the days of steam ships.

The National Trust owns many fine orangeries – at Saltram in Devon, at Tatton Park in Cheshire, at Calke Abbey (where funds are being sought to rebuild the orangery which overlooks the erstwhile vegetable garden). At Wallington, in Northumberland, and at Felbrigg orangeries have become conservatories as well, filled with fine flowering plants in the Victorian tradition. At Clumber Park in Nottinghamshire, the restored conservatory has a splendid collection of wall-grown figs, nectarines and grapes.

The passion for growing tender and demanding fruit against all the odds created by the English climate meant that much money and effort went into growing melons and pineapples, even bananas at Petworth House in Sussex, although the experiment was not entirely successful. The often related story is that Henry, 2nd Lord Leconfield, built a special glasshouse and sent his gardener up to Kew to learn how to grow bananas, having been told that they tasted so much better straight from the tree. On ceremoniously tasting the first of this fruit, which had cost £3,000 to produce, he was disgusted to find that it tasted exactly like any other.

J. C. Loudon, the nineteenth-century horticulturalist, gives pages of directions for growing pineapples, because, he says: 'The fruit reckoned the most delicious of all others, and gardeners being valued by the wealthy in proportion to their success in its cultivation.' Although the well-known picture which hangs at Ham House shows Charles II being presented with the first pineapple ever grown in England, in about 1677, it was not until 1753 that Richard Bradley gave the first pineapple recipe to appear in an English cookery book. His recipe for 'A Tart of the Ananas, or Pineapple. From Barbadoes' is very good indeed.

RICHARD BRADLEY'S PINEAPPLE TART

1 medium-sized pineapple	1 8in (20cm) flan case made of sweet
$\frac{1}{4}$pt (150ml) madeira	shortcrust pastry
1 tablespoon (15ml) brown sugar	(see p.101)
	$\frac{1}{4}$pt (150ml) double cream (optional)

Cut away the peel from the pineapple, reserving the tuft of leaves for decoration, and cut out all the 'knots'. Cut into slices about $\frac{1}{2}$in (1.25cm) thick, then core each slice and cut into quarters. Cook these pieces very gently in the madeira and sugar until soft – about 15 minutes – and leave to cool. Arrange the fruit in the flan case, pour the syrup over, put the tart into the oven on a heated baking tray and bake for about 25 minutes at 350°F, 180°C; gas mark 4. 'When it comes from the Oven, pour Cream over it, (if you have it) and serve it either hot or cold.' If you are serving it cold, trim the base of the tuft of leaves and arrange it in the centre of the tart – it gives the necessary eighteenth-century grandeur.

Recipes for preserving green pineapples seemed to be as necessary as for preserving green oranges, grapes or peaches. This is Mrs Raffald's recipe, which assumes that there will be vine leaves on hand as well – which was a safe assumption since vines were frequently grown alongside the more tropical fruit. These were used to help keep the fruit green which otherwise went a dreary yellowish colour during cooking, but I have not had much success with this method.

TO PRESERVE GREEN PINE-APPLES

Get your pine-apples before they are ripe, and lay them in strong salt and water five days, then put a large handful of vine-leaves in the bottom of a large sauce-pan, and put in your pine-apples, fill your pan with vine-leaves, then pour on the salt and water it was laid in, cover it up very close, and set it over a slow fire, let it stand till it is a fine light green, have ready a thin syrup, made of a quart of water and a pound of double-refined sugar; when it is almost cold put it into a deep jar, and put in the pine-apple with the top on, let it stand a week, and take care that it is well covered with the syrup, then boil your syrup again, and pour it carefully into your jar, lest you break the top of your pine-apple, and let it stand eight or ten weeks, and give the syrup two or three boils to keep it from moulding, let your syrup stand till it is near cold before you pour it on; when your pine-apple looks quite full and green, take it out of the syrup, and make a thick syrup of three pounds of double-refined sugar with as much water as will dissolve it, boil and skim it well, put a few slices of white ginger in it; when it is near cold, pour it upon your pine-apple, tie it down with a bladder, and the pine-apple will keep many years, and not shrink; but if you put into thick syrup at the first, it will shrink, for the strength of the syrup draws out the juice, and spoils it.

A quicker method, for preserving slices rather than the whole fruit, is as follows:

Preserved Pineapple

Cut a large pineapple into thick slices, core and then trim each to get rid of the spines. Weigh the fruit at this point and calculate 1lb (450g) sugar to each pound of fruit. Dissolve some of the sugar in $\frac{1}{4}$ pint (150ml) water, then add the rest of the sugar; melt slowly, then boil to a syrup. Add the pineapple slices and simmer for $\frac{1}{2}$ hour or until they are transparent and tender. Pot in preserving jars. Pineapple preserved in this way is very good for adding to cakes, and can make a delicious and luxurious stuffing for baked apples.

It is quite likely that pineapples were grown in the magnificent range of glasshouses still to be seen at Clumber Park (which also houses a fine collection of garden implements), since plants were flourishing all over the country by the time these were built in the late nineteenth century. It is hardly surprising that the Trust doesn't devote its energies to producing the fruit these days. Despite the reassurance of one Victorian gardening book that the pineapple 'is more easily brought to maturity than an early cucumber', nevertheless the cost of heating the greenhouse to 'the high temperature requisite for the pine in every stage of its growth, renders it necessary to have recourse to fire-heat for eight or nine months in every year', prohibitive in these days of expensive fuel. Even the water for watering the plants had to be kept warm: 'I would advise never to water them with water under seventy (degrees), unless in very warm weather.' It is easy to see that the pineapple was a status symbol, much as a swimming pool might be today.

Hot-house fruit formed the centrepiece of many an Edwardian or Victorian dessert; the pineapple would take centre stage, resting on vine leaves, perhaps rivalled by a fine melon 'which should have the stalk showing at the top', says Mrs Beeton, who devotes several pages to the arrangement of fruit. Grapes looked best when red and white were displayed together, 'drooping a little over the edge of the stand, which should be one upon a stem, and this, if tall, may have a spray of climbing fern or other creeper twined round it'. Sometimes, small fruits were displayed *en chemise*, or dipped in beaten egg white, then in sugar and left to dry so that they looked frosted. Grapes, cherries and white and red currants look very pretty like this. Mrs Beeton felt that perfectly ripe nectarines, figs, peaches and apricots were so beautifully coloured that they needed nothing more than a few green leaves to set them off.

Richard Bradley suggested growing vines in pots in the greenhouse, so that 'it is easy to conceive how pleasant it will be to have them thus brought growing to the Table in a Dessert' – a charming idea, which reached a peak of absurdity, however, during the Edwardian era. Having mastered the art of the 'table vine', a miniature fruit-bearing vine from which the ladies could cut their own bunches at dessert, it was thought necessary to invent an even more elaborately 'natural' scene by appearing to have the vine grow up through the table itself. This meant producing a specially constructed top with a hole in it, and presumably tablecloths to match.

Hot-house grapes were skilfully stored well into the winter by cutting each bunch with a good length of stalk and keeping them in bottles filled with water and a little charcoal to keep it fresh. The bottles were stored in racks and the grapes kept for months. I have once tasted muscat grapes kept like this and the flavour was unforgettable; it was deep, sweet and aromatic, the fruit only just beginning to wrinkle a little, but otherwise plump and juicy – and this was at New Year after the grapes had been stored since early September.

The National Trust has several properties where grapes can be seen. At Beningbrough Hall, Mr Walker, the Head Gardener, is proud of two vines which were bred there in 1835 by the then Head Gardener, Thomas Foster. Foster's Seedling and Lady Downe's Seedling still flourish there, although the present plants are cuttings from the originals. The wonderfully restored conservatory at Clumber Park houses grapes as well as nectarines, peaches and figs, and at The Courts in Wiltshire, the charming eighteenth-century conservatory contains vines.

There are many recipes which make use of green grapes, suggesting that many vines grew out of doors and so held a mass of unripened fruit. Verjuice was a condiment often used in early recipes – a sharp, vinegar-like seasoning made from unripe grapes. It can be imitated by using a very dry white wine with a little white wine vinegar added. For interest's sake, and for those who have plenty of grapes which have not ripened by the start of winter, here is an eighteenth-century recipe for making it.

To Make Verjuice of Grapes

Take Grapes full grown, just before they begin to ripen, and bruise them, without the trouble of picking them from the Bunches; then put them in a Bag, made of Horse-Hair, and press them till the Juice is discharged; put this Liquor into a Stone Jar, leaving it uncover'd for some Days, then close it and keep it for use. NB Keep this in a good Vault, and it will remain good for three or four Years as Verjuice; but a little more time will make it lose its Sourness, and it will become like Wine.

Verjuice was used to great effect in sauces for rich meat, such as goose or pork. It is used in this seventeenth-century recipe by Gervase Markham.

Sauce for a Pig

Take sage and roast it in the belly of the Pig; then boyling Verjuyce, Butter, and Currants together, take and chop the sage small, and mixing the brains of the Pig with it, put all together and so serve it up.

Brains added to a gravy for roast sucking pig might not be popular today, but if that recipe is translated into a gravy made with the juices left in the roasting tin after cooking a joint of pork with plenty of sage, to which dry white wine and a thread of vinegar are added, the recipe sounds more palatable and is very good. The currants add a pleasant sweetness.

A much later recipe – Mrs Beeton's for Grape Jam – specifically calls for unripe grapes, and is again very useful for using up fruit which has not ripened by the end of the season.

Grape Jam

Check the unripe grapes carefully, picking them off their stalks and throwing out any which are blemished. Weigh them when they have been prepared and washed and calculate 8oz (225g) sugar to each pound of grapes. Layer the grapes and sugar in a preserving pan (beginning with a layer of grapes) and put on a low heat without any water. When the sugar has melted, bring quickly to the boil and boil until the setting point has been reached – in about half-an-hour.

The advantage of using unripe grapes is that the pips are hardly formed and so do not need to be removed; the snag is that the flavour is equally unformed and the jam can be a little lacking in character. The following recipe for Grape Jelly calls for ripe, black grapes and is very good indeed.

Grape Jelly

Prepare the grapes as above and put them in a preserving pan, again without water and this time without sugar either. Cook gently until they burst and release the juice. Strain overnight through a jelly bag. Next day, weigh the juice (weigh an empty bowl on the scales, then pour in the juice and calculate the difference). Pour the juice into the preserving pan add 14oz (400g) sugar for each pound of juice. Boil to setting point (after about 15 minutes), skimming well, and pot.

But by far the best recipes are for oranges and lemons, which have long been used in the most imaginative ways. Citrus fruit grown in elegant English orangeries needs plenty of sun to ripen it; fruit may form, but without sun it will never ripen to any sweetness. Most of the recipes, therefore, are for candied or preserved fruit; the following produces a mildly rum-flavoured syrup and rich, sweet, whole fruit which can be cut into quarters and served with other desserts.

PRESERVED ORANGES AND LEMONS

4 thin-skinned oranges *sugar*
2 thin-skinned lemons *rum*
water

Scrub the fruit very well to get rid of any wax (unless you are able to buy unwaxed fruit), and put in a large pan which will hold them comfortably. Measure the amount of water necessary to cover them by 1in (2.5cm), then add 2lb (900g) preserving sugar to each pint of water. Heat until the sugar dissolves, then raise the heat and bring to the boil. Reduce the heat and simmer gently until the fruit is soft and the syrup reduced by half. When cold, pack the fruit into preserving jars, and add 1 wineglassful of rum to every pint of syrup and top up the jars – tap each jar to get rid of any air bubbles. Cap tightly and store in a cool, dark place. If the syrup begins to thin, reboil it with more sugar and add more rum if liked.

PRESERVED ORANGE CREAM

6 large oranges *½pt (250ml) double*
1 lemon *cream*
water *4oz (125g) preserved*
1oz (25g) gelatine *orange, chopped*
sugar to taste

Grate the rind from the oranges and lemon, then squeeze the juice from the fruit and add water to bring the amount of liquid up to 1½ pints (750ml). Put the juice, rinds, gelatine and sugar to taste into a pan over a low heat for 10 minutes. Strain, cool, and when just beginning to set add the cream – this is best done in the liquidiser. Fold in the preserved orange and pour into a bowl to set. Decorate with slivers of preserved orange, and small leaves frosted (see page 103).

PRESERVED ORANGE AND LEMON PEEL

Scrub oranges and lemons very well, then peel and remove as much of the pith from the inside as possible by scraping with a sharp knife. Chop the peel fairly finely – in a food processor if necessary – but do not let it become too fine. Layer the peels in a preserving jar with a good sprinkling of sugar between each layer (you can add more peel and sugar to the jar as you go along), then cap tightly. Shake as often as you can remember. The sugar turns to syrup, and the peel is good for cakes and puddings; grapefruit is very good kept this way.

At Dyrham Park, between Bath and Bristol, teas are served in the fine orangery designed at the turn of the seventeenth century by William Talman, Sir Christopher Wren's rival at Hampton Court. This teabread recipe is on the menu, appropriately, and is delicious; the preserved peel made by the above process works very well as a substitute for the mixed peel.

DYRHAM BITTER ORANGE TEABREAD

rind of 2 oranges,
  coarsely grated
4fl oz (100ml) orange
  juice
4oz (125g) mixed or
  preserved peel,
  chopped
4oz (125g) margarine

3oz (75g) light
  muscovado sugar
1 egg
3oz (75g) self-raising
  flour
3oz (75g) wholemeal
  flour

Grease a 1lb (450g) loaf tin. Mix together the orange rind and juice and the peel. Cream the margarine and sugar until light and fluffy. Beat in the egg accompanied by 2 tablespoons (30ml) flour, add half the remaining flour with half the orange mixture and fold in carefully with a metal spoon. Add the remaining flour and the rest of the orange mixture and mix well. Spoon into the prepared tin and bake at 350°F, 180°C; gas mark 4 for about 1 hour, or until the cake is beginning to leave the sides of the tin. Cool for 5 minutes, then turn on to a rack.

Peckover House, a restrained and elegant Georgian town house in Wisbech, has an orangery which is anything but restrained. It is filled with myriads of flowering pot plants, which surround three venerable orange trees planted in troughs. These trees regularly bear fruit, Mr Underwood, the Head Gardener, tells me, and need only a minimum temperature of 45°F (7°C) throughout the winter – which means that similarly successful fruiting might be expected of any tree in a sunny conservatory (and a much more attainable goal than raising pineapples).

Eighteenth-century directions for growing oranges suggest that the trees may safely be brought out of their winter shelter by the time that the leaves on the mulberry 'are as large as a crow's foot, which, perhaps, may be a certain Sign of the settled Temperature of the Air', although a note of doubt is apparent here. The directions go on to warn of overwatering, and that sudden drenches of cold water should be avoided. The trees should be pruned in February, trimming the shoots of the preceding summer to 6 inches (15cm). Then, 'if they are discreetly made acquainted with the external Air, before they are set out of the House', they will make good new growth.

The beautiful orangery at Saltram is as full of citrus fruit now as it probably was soon after it was built in 1775. The trees are in pots and are moved to their summer quarters when the weather is warm enough, to surround a nearby pool and fountain and make a very pleasant citrus grove.

The following recipe, although it is from Mrs Beeton and is therefore Victorian, is in the style of the Georgian 'transparent' tarts, in a baking dish edged, but not lined, with puff pastry. It calls for Seville or bitter oranges, but it can equally well be made with sweet oranges, in which case add the grated rind of one of the lemons.

SEVILLE ORANGE PUDDING

4 Seville oranges
juice of 2 lemons
grated rind of 1 lemon
  (optional, see above)
6oz (175g) unsalted
  butter

12 almonds, blanched and
  chopped
8oz (225g) caster sugar
8 eggs
3oz (75g) puff pastry

Boil the oranges until soft, then chop them finely, taking care to remove all the pips. Put the pulp in a basin with all the other ingredients except the eggs and pastry; stand the basin over a pan of hot water until the butter and sugar have melted. Beat well. Cool a little, then add the very well-beaten eggs. Roll out the puff pastry, cut it into strips and edge a baking dish with it. Pour the orange mixture into the dish and bake for 40 minutes in a moderate oven or until set.

Dunster Castle, near Minehead, boasts a pair of aged lemon trees which produce good crops of lemons with nothing but the protection of a cold frame in the hardest weather. It seems fitting to match lemons with fish here, since the mild maritime climate enables these particular trees to flourish. The recipe is based on an early Victorian one, and it is a wonderful sauce for any fish which might have a tendency to dryness, such as salmon or halibut.

Lemon Butter Sauce

6oz (175g) slightly	*2 lemons*
salted butter	*salt*

Cut the butter into cubes (about 1in [2.5cm] square) and chill it in the fridge. Grate the rind of roughly a quarter of one of the lemons and put it in a small basin. Peel the rest of the lemon very thickly, cutting away all the pith, and dice the flesh as small as possible, getting rid of the pips as you go. Put the diced flesh in the basin with the rind, together with the juice of the remaining lemon. Stand the basin over a pan of simmering water and allow the mixture to get very hot. Remove the pan from the heat and whisk in the butter, a cube at a time. It should melt to a cream, and not 'oil' as the old books call it. If the mixture cools too much to melt the butter, return the pan to a low heat and continue to whisk. When all the butter has been incorporated, check the seasoning and add salt if necessary. Remove the bowl from the pan and transfer the sauce to a warm sauceboat. Serve at once.

Another West Country National Trust property, Cotehele, near the mouth of the Tamar in Cornwall, serves a delicious lemonade which often makes a welcome alternative to tea on hot summer afternoons. It is so easy to make, and keeps so well, that it is worth making in some quantity.

Cotehele Lemonade

3 lemons	*1oz (25g) citric acid*
1½lb (675g) sugar	*2pt (1.25l) boiling water*

Grate or peel the lemons thinly, then halve and squeeze out the juice. Put juice, peel, sugar and citric acid into a large bowl and pour over the boiling water, stirring until all the sugar has dissolved. Cover and leave to cool completely. Strain into a large jug and bottle in clean, dry bottles. Dilute to taste.

NB Use this same method to make elderflower lemonade, by adding half a dozen heads of the flowers to the bowl with the rest of the ingredients. Leave to infuse overnight.

The next recipe is an adaptation of a recipe which dates from the end of the seventeenth century, but remained popular for some time. I have adapted it only in that I use a leg of lamb rather than the suggested shoulder, and use half the amount of claret.

To Roste Mutton with Lemmons

1 leg of lamb
2 lemons
salt and pepper
freshly grated nutmeg
pinch of ginger
$\frac{1}{2}$pt (250ml) lamb stock
  (made from the end
  bone, or use a lamb stock
  cube as a compromise)

$\frac{1}{2}$pt (250ml) claret, or
  other full-bodied red
  wine
1 dessertspoon (10ml)
  white wine vinegar

Make incisions all over the leg of lamb. Peel one of the lemons thinly, cut four slices from the other for the garnish, then squeeze the juice from both of them. Pour some of the lemon juice over the lamb, season it with salt, pepper, a little nutmeg and ginger, and roast it for 20 minutes per pound in a moderate oven (375°F, 190°C; gas mark 5), basting it from time to time with more lemon juice.

Meanwhile, cut the lemon rind into fine julienne strips, cover with cold water and bring to the boil. Simmer for 5 minutes, then throw away the water and repeat with a fresh lot. Drain and reserve. When the lamb is ready, carve it in thick slices and arrange on a heated serving dish, and keep it warm while you make the sauce: drain any fat from the pan, and pour in the heated stock and the wine. Bring to the boil, scraping up all the bits which have stuck to the bottom of the pan and simmer to reduce the liquid and allow the flavours to blend. Add the vinegar, simmer for another 5 minutes, then strain the sauce into a clean pan. Add the strips of lemon rind, check the seasoning, and pour over the slices of lamb. Garnish with the slices of lemon, notched around the edge, and serve very hot.

Lemon and orange syllabubs were served in small glasses at many an eighteenth-century entertainment. Deceptively innocent, they are extremely alcoholic and should be served with care to drivers. This recipe is adapted from Hannah Glasse.

To Make Whipt Syllabubs

$\frac{1}{4}$pt (150ml) madeira
1pt (500ml) double
  cream
$\frac{1}{4}$pt (150ml) white wine

2oz (50g) caster sugar
juice and grated peel of
  1 lemon

Divide the madeira between 8 small glasses. Whip the cream with the wine, sugar, lemon juice and peel until thick, then spoon it into the glasses. Decorate with ratafias, or angelica, or preserved orange or lemon.

If the fruit from these trees was not always forthcoming, the blossom in May was usually copious. The scent of orange and lemon blossom is well known, and many old recipes as well as modern ones call for orange-flower water. But there are recipes for using the flowers in other ways, and one of my favourites is to set them in an orange-flavoured apple jelly, as a delicate alternative to marmalade for breakfast. The recipe is Richard Bradley's.

TO PRESERVE ORANGE FLOWERS IN JELLY

*juice and peel of
    4 oranges
2lb (900g) Bramley
    apples
2pt (1.25l) water
sugar*

*1 large cupful of orange
    flowers, fresh or dried
    (dried orange flowers
    are available from
    Culpeper Ltd, see
    p.114)*

Peel the oranges thinly, then squeeze out the juice. Put the juice and peel in a large pan, with the apples cut in chunks (do not peel or core) and the water. Bring to the boil and cook until the apples are soft and pulpy. Tip into a jelly bag or pillowcase and allow to drain overnight. Next day, measure the juice and add 1lb (450g) sugar to each pint (500ml) liquid. Bring to the boil and cook to setting point.

While the jelly is boiling, prepare the orange flowers: if using fresh ones (Bradley directs 'Gather your Orange-Flowers, in the Morning early, when they are just open'), nip off the end of each flower. Cover with cold water, bring rapidly to the boil, then drain and refresh in cold water. Repeat this twice. If using dried flowers, pour hot but not boiling water over them and leave to infuse and soften, then drain. When the jelly is ready, draw the pan off the heat and leave to cool for 15–20 minutes. Stir in the orange flowers, then pot and cover in the usual way. If you add the flowers when the jelly is still very hot, they will simply float to the top of the jar; by waiting for the jelly to cool, they will be suspended throughout the jelly once potted. If you have no orange flowers to hand, either fresh or dried, then add a generous tablespoonful (15ml) of orange-flower water to the jelly half way through its cooking time.

Finally, an Edwardian or Victorian 'conceit' found in many cookery books of the period and fun to make on a wet afternoon. As preparing the orange shells takes some time, using packet jellies will speed the process although real fruit jelly made according to the recipe on p.103 is preferable; in the Edwardian kitchen, one kitchen maid would have spent time preparing the shells, the other would have been entrusted with preparing the jellies from fresh fruit and isinglass – a scene easily imagined in the magnificent kitchens at Lanhydrock.

ORANGES FILLED WITH JELLY

4 large oranges
1 packet strawberry or
   raspberry jelly, made
   up with orange juice
1 packet lemon jelly, with
   lemon juice added to the
   water when making up

well-shaped fresh green
   leaves – bay, rose, or
   orange or lemon leaves
   if available

Cut a piece the size of a 20p piece from the stalk end of each orange and hollow out the flesh using a teaspoon handle. Soak the shells in cold water for an hour after which the fibrous pith should come away fairly easily when scraped with a finger nail. Try to avoid piercing the orange skins.

Soak in cold water again to harden the skins, and then drain upside down while you make up the jellies as directed on the packet, but using a little less liquid to obtain a really firm set. Check the orange shells for any tears (you can patch these up fairly successfully with waterproof sticking plaster), then stand each shell in a cup. Pour in the jelly, two strawberry and two lemon, or you can stripe the jelly by pouring in first one colour and leaving it to set, and then the other, continuing until the oranges are full. Leave the jelly to set absolutely firm.

Next day, find a decorative serving dish, one with a stem if possible. With a very sharp, long-bladed knife, cut each orange in quarters. Arrange in a pyramid, alternating the colours or, if you have striped the jelly, arrange so that the stripes are shown off to best advantage. Decorate with the leaves.

A Compendium of Useful Hints

A Compendium of
Useful Hints

TRUE sign of good housewifery has always been a well-filled larder; shelves of shining jars of preserves and pickles, crocks of salted beans, perhaps eggs in waterglass and barrels of butter. Traditionally, dried herbs would have hung, not in picturesque bunches from hooks in the kitchen ceiling, but bagged in muslin to keep off dust, and in a cool dry dark place away from the heat of cooking and the daylight that destroys the flavour. With all the bounty of the summer to be carefully stored to see the household through the winter, it isn't surprising that larders and store cupboards were considered important, and were as roomy as possible.

Modern storage has now been restricted to the larder fridge, the freezer and a range of cupboards that the Victorian housewife would have considered extremely skimpy. Preservation, no longer as necessary since strawberries and asparagus can be obtained at Christmas and leeks at midsummer, is usually simply a matter of preparing vegetables for the freezer.

This is a pity, since many of the old methods of preservation are good dishes in themselves. A jam is more useful and interesting than a bagful of frozen plums, and a cordial of blackcurrants can become a sauce for roast duck or for ice-cream, a long cold drink on a hot day, or a short hot one to pamper 'flu. A jar of bottled damsons can be topped with a crumble mix to make an instant pudding, or can simply be emptied into a decorative dish, sprinkled with some toasted almonds and be served up at a dinner party without any apology.

It is worth looking at some of these old methods of prolonging the useful life of seasonal vegetables, fruit, herbs and even flowers. I am not suggesting that it is necessary to revert to using wax to seal jars when there are modern versions around. Various types of patent preserving jars are still widely available, of which Kilner, the best known, have been joined by their French counterparts,

called Le Parfait, in many fashionable kitchen shops. Muslin bags
for dried herbs can be made from old sheeting, along the lines of a
shoe bag, with a drawstring top and the name of the herb written
in marking ink on the outside, unless you have time to embroider
it. Alternatively, dark glass jars, such as those which held instant
coffee or beef extract, are ideal, since they exclude light. Clear
glass might look delightful, but the herbs quickly lose their colour
and flavour when exposed to light.

WHEN TO GATHER HERBS FOR DRYING

It is meet that our Housewife know that from the eight of the
Kalends of the month of April, unto the eight of the Kalends
of July, all manner of herbs and leaves are in that time most in
strength and of the greatest vertue to be used, and put in all
manner of Medicines, also from the eight of the Kalends of
July, unto the eight of the Kalends of October, the Stalkes,
stems and hard branches of every herb and plant is most in
strength to be used in Medicines; and from the eight of the
Kalends of October, unto the eight of the Kalends of April,
all manner of roots of herbs and plants are most of the
strength and virtue to be used in all manner of Medicines.

Gervase Markham's advice is as sound for herbs used in cooking as
in medicine – gather the leaves first, before the plants flower, then
the stalks, in late summer. Fennel is the most useful of all the herb
stems to dry, as they can be used to flavour fish soups and stews,
and are particularly good used as a bed on which to grill pork
chops. Roots such as horseradish and Hamburg parsley (much
favoured by Victorian cooks) can be dug up throughout the
winter if the weather allows.

Harvest the herbs on a dry day, when the sun has dried any
moisture on the plants, and spread them out on newspaper in a
warm dry place – an airing cupboard, or on a sunny windowsill.
Turn them frequently, especially if the season has been a wet one,
until they are completely dry and friable. Rub the leaves from the
stems and store them in dark glass jars, as described above. Do not
throw away the stalks, since those of thyme, marjoram and
rosemary are useful for flavouring winter soups and stews, or for
arranging round a roasting chicken or leg of lamb.

WINTER BOUQUET GARNI

Take a large piece of celery and break it in half. Use the halves
to sandwich together a mixture of herb stalks and a bay leaf

or two, plus a strip of orange or lemon peel. Tie with string, leaving a long piece to tie to the handle of the pan you are cooking in so that the bouquet can be fished out and discarded once it has done its work.

An old method of storing dried bay leaves was to include a small piece of cotton rag soaked in a flavourless oil (sunflower or grapeseed) in the jar with the leaves. This was, I suppose, to keep the bayleaves pliable, and it certainly succeeds, but the oil does go rancid so the old rag should be thrown out and replaced after about three months.

Dried herbs can be made up into various blends, as that on page 104. Here is another one, from Francatelli's *The Cook's Guide*, called 'Herbaceous Seasoning', which includes spices.

Herbaceous Seasoning

Take of nutmegs and mace 1oz of each; of cloves and peppercorns 2oz of each; 1oz dried bay leaves, 3oz dried basil, the same of marjoram, 2oz winter savoury, 3oz thyme, $\frac{1}{2}$oz of cayenne, the same of grated lemon peel, and 2 cloves of garlic; all these ingredients must be well pulverised in a mortar and sifted through a fine wire sieve, and put away in dry corked bottles for use.

This is worth making in large quantities, as a small jar makes a welcome present. The mortar has been replaced, luckily, by the food processor; blend all the ingredients until as fine as possible, sift them on to sheets of paper and dry off in a warm oven overnight, allow to become cold before putting into jars. It makes a particularly good seasoning for steak and kidney pie, oxtail and game dishes.

Herb oils and vinegars are another good way of prolonging the scents of summer. To make either, simply gather the herbs when they are at their most aromatic (see above) and add two or three sprigs to about a pint (500ml) of oil or vinegar. Cap tightly and stand in the sun for a week or so, or until the liquid is well flavoured. Strain out the herbs, rebottle and label, then store in a cool dark place.

The following mixtures are particularly effective:

Basil leaves in red wine vinegar – to add in small quantities to brown stews, to the gravy to partner beef, and to lentil dishes.

Lemon peel and fennel seeds to white wine or cider vinegar – to add to court bouillon for cooking fish, to season mayonnaise to go with salmon or chicken.

Sprigs of tarragon in a mild olive oil – to dribble over fish before baking in the oven, and to dress any lettuce, tomato or potato salad.

Halved cloves of young garlic, sprigs of rosemary and oregano in extra virgin olive oil – to use to baste grilled or barbecued meat, for roast lamb and chicken, beef and veal, or to brush over slices of French bread before toasting, to serve with fish soups.

One of my favourite flavourings comes from Anne Cobbett's *The English Housekeeper* (1851).

Basil Wine

About the end of August fill a wide-mouthed bottle with fresh leaves of basil, cover with Sherry, and infuse them ten days; strain and put in fresh leaves, infuse another ten days, then pour off, and bottle it; A tablespoonful to a tureen of mock turtle, just before it is served.

It is equally good in tomato or game soups, and makes a wonderful addition to the gravy for roast beef.

Flowers were preserved to add to salads in the seventeenth century, adding a sweet note which would be unfamiliar to us today. Candied flowers keep very well, however, and are fun to make and can look very decorative on cakes and desserts. Candied violets are the most familiar, and they certainly taste good, but their decorative merits are not as valuable as those of simpler flowers. Primroses, single roses, most fruit blossom, *clematis montana*, all have simple outlines which are not blurred by the sugar – I have even used the single flowers of azaleas when decorating a late spring birthday cake – and of course any well-shaped leaves are ideal subjects. A Christmas cake looks beautiful decorated with candied ivy leaves, and there is a tip for frosting holly leaves on page 113; just make sure that no one is tempted by the sugar coating to eat them.

The best method is to use gum arabic, an edible gum which can be obtained from chemists, or from cake decoration specialists. Dissolve it, at the rate of 1 oz per $\frac{1}{4}$ pint (25g per 150ml), in warm water. Make sure that the leaves and flowers are absolutely dry, then dip them in the gum solution and then in caster sugar; shake gently to get rid of surplus sugar. Arrange them on a baking sheet or tray lined with baking parchment and leave to dry in an airing cupboard until set. These can be stored for some time in an airtight plastic box kept in a dry, cool place.

If no gum arabic is available, egg white can be used instead. Beat egg whites until frothy, then proceed as above. Flowers candied by this method will not keep as long, and are best used as soon as they are dry – prepare on the day before you need them so that they have time to set overnight.

Preserving vegetables was a risky business, as botulism, one of the most deadly of food poisonings, could result from a faulty seal. Salting is one of the ways of avoiding such a risk, and almost every household had its crock of salted green beans 'put down' for the winter. These beans have their fans, although I am not one, so I include the method here, taking it straight from the *Cookery Book of Lady Clark of Tillypronie* (1909):

FRENCH, OR KIDNEY BEANS – TO PRESERVE

Slice them or leave them whole; have a large basin or crock; lay in it salt an inch deep; on that put a layer of beans, then salt again, and so on – but cover the top layer of beans with salt, and they will keep well. When wanted, they are boiled like fresh beans, but you change the water when the beans are half cooked. The Druminnor butler bottles beans with salt, and corks them up to exclude the air.

Pickling was the most popular way of preserving vegetables. In the seventeenth century anything and everything was drowned in vinegar in order to lengthen the season – cucumber, samphire, broom and nasturtium buds, and so on – and then served as part of the popular elaborate 'Compound Sallets'. Anne Cobbett gives a 'pickling table' in *The English Housekeeper*:

PICKLING SEASONS

Artichokes are in season in July & August
Cauliflowers in July & August
Capsicum pods, end of July & beginning of August
Cucumbers, the end of July to the end of August
French beans, July
Mushrooms, September
Nasturtium pods, middle of July

Onions from the middle to the end of July
Radish pods, July
Red cabbage, August
Samphire, August
Tomatoes, the end of July to the end of August.

Coarser variants survive in the form of pickled onions, red cabbage and piccalilli. This recipe for pickled Brussels sprouts is more unusual.

Pickled Brussels Sprouts

*1 lb (450g) small tight
    very fresh sprouts
2oz (50g) fine sea salt
1 pint (500ml) white
    malt vinegar*

*1 tablespoon (15ml)
    mixed pickling spices
1oz (25g) sugar*

Trim the sprouts, spread them in a flat dish and sprinkle them with the salt, then leave overnight. Next day, rinse them, drain well and pack them into a large clean dry jar. Put the vinegar, spices and sugar in a saucepan, bring to the boil, simmer briskly for 10 minutes, then pour this mixture over the sprouts in their jar. Allow to become absolutely cold before putting on the lids, which should be plastic as vinegar will corrode metal. Eat within about 2 months.

Onions, garlic and shallots are best stored with a good current of air round them. The old method which is as good as any is to plait the stems together so that they can be hung up. Knot together three strands of string or raffia, about 2 feet long. Take three onions, twist the withered stems round the string and plait these tightly together twice; repeat with another set of three and continue until the string has been used up but leaving enough to tie the ends together. Treat shallots and garlic in the same way.

The art of bottling fruit has almost disappeared, which is a pity. A jar of gooseberries in elderflower syrup can be translated into a gooseberry fool, a sorbet, a pie, a crumble or a sauce in minutes, with no tiresome defrosting to delay matters. Furthermore, bottled fruit costs nothing to keep, survives power cuts, lasts for several years, looks attractive on the larder shelf and makes good presents, especially if the syrups are flavoured to complement the fruit. I give the basic method on page 61, but here are a few flavourings that add interest:

Grated orange rind, orange juice and honey to rhubarb
Madeira or sweet sherry to plums
Pieces of vanilla pod to apricots
Pieces of cinnamon stick to damsons
Scented geranium leaves to blackberries and blackcurrants
Elderberries to apple purée
Strips of lemon peel to peaches
A few cloves and a piece of root ginger to pears
Elderflowers to gooseberries
Cinnamon and cloves to orange slices

Herb and fruit cordials were made in their due season, and doubled both as refreshment and medication. Some were simply syrups while others owed their keeping qualities to the large amounts of alcohol used in their composition. I give recipes throughout the book for such restoratives as lavender drops (page 24) and hop tonic (page 25), and liqueurs like raspberry brandy (page 70) and Loudon's Admirable (page 84), but the recipe that follows caps them all. It was given to me by a friend while we were living at Styal and appeared in a book I was writing at the time. It is an old family recipe that cleverly preserves all the fresh flavour and possibly all the vitamin C content of a large quantity of oranges and lemons by adding their juice to a powerfully spicy syrup.

GINGERETTE

4pt (2.5l) water
2lb (900g) demerara
    sugar
1oz (25g) whole cloves
1½oz (37g) dried chillies
1½oz (37g) root ginger,
    bruised

1oz (25g) cinnamon
    sticks
10 oranges
8 lemons
cochineal for colouring
    (optional)

Tie the spices up in a piece of muslin and put them in a large, heavy pan together with the sugar and water. Dissolve the sugar over a low heat, bring to a full boil, then lower the heat and simmer for 1½ hours. Remove from the heat and take out the bag of spices, then leave the syrup to cool while you squeeze the juice from the fruit. Strain this into the warm syrup, then colour prettily with the cochineal if you like. Bottle when cold. Dilute with hot or cold water to make a winter or summer drink, and add a shot of brandy or whisky for extra warmth on a cold day.

APPENDIX

The recipes in this section are of general use throughout the book.

The following recipe is ideal for all fruit tarts using uncooked fruit, ie strawberries, raspberries, mulberries, etc.

PÂTE SUCRÉE FLAN CASES

9oz (260g) plain flour
pinch of salt
3 tablespoons (45ml)
  icing sugar
6oz (175g) unsalted
  butter

1 tablespoon (15ml)
  water
3 drops real vanilla
  essence
1 egg yolk for glazing

Butter two flan tins with removeable bases sparingly but thoroughly. Sieve the flour, salt and icing sugar into a bowl. Melt the butter with the water over a low heat and pour straight on to the flour mixture, adding the vanilla essence at the same time, and mix to a soft dough with a wooden spoon. Immediately divide the dough into two and press it over the bases of the flan cases and up the sides. Patch any cracks, and try to avoid a thick area where the sides join the base. To produce neat edges, run a rolling pin across the tops of the flan tins. Refrigerate for at least one hour, then preheat oven to 400°F, 200°C; gas mark 7, line the cases with non-stick baking parchment and ceramic baking beans and bake for 15 minutes. Remove beans and paper, brush the inside of the flan cases with egg yolk and return to the oven until a deep gold. Optionally, glaze the cases with jam to match the fruit.

CRISP SHORTCRUST PASTRY

This shortcrust pastry comes into its own when eaten cold, since the milk adds to the fat content and therefore to the crispness. It is ideal for pies, and for tarts where the filling is cooked with the case.

8oz (220g) plain flour
4oz (125g) butter

very cold milk to mix

Rub the butter into the flour and mix to a dough with the milk. Chill for half an hour before using. NB For sweet pastry, use unsalted butter and 1 tbsp (15ml) icing sugar.

CRÊME PATISSIÈRE

This pastry cream makes an excellent base for fruit flans and tarts, not as rich as whipped cream, but light and just as good at offsetting the sharp sweetness of the fruit.

2 egg yolks   *1¼oz (35g) cornflour*
2oz (50g) vanilla sugar   *½pt (250ml) milk*
* (see p.102)*   *1 egg white*

Whisk the egg yolks and sugar in a basin, mix the cornflour with about a quarter of the milk and put the rest of the milk in a pan to heat until almost boiling. Blend the cornflour with the egg yolks, then pour on the hot milk gradually, stirring all the time. Return the mixture to the pan over a medium heat and stir until it thickens and coats the back of a spoon. Draw off the heat. Whip the egg white until stiff, then fold it into the custard in the pan, return to a very low heat and cook for a further 2–3 minutes. Turn into a basin and cool. For extra richness, fold in $\frac{1}{4}$ pint (150ml) whipped whipping cream just before using.

VANILLA SUGAR

Vanilla sugar makes all the difference to sweet dishes, and is very good sprinkled on sliced fresh strawberries or on to raspberries. Simply add two vanilla pods, cut into 2in (5cm) lengths, to a large jar of caster sugar. Top up the sugar as it is used. The pieces of vanilla pod can be used for flavouring custards or milk puddings, or for cooking with apricots and sweet dessert apples. After using, wash them under a hot tap, dry on kitchen paper and return them to the jar of sugar.

Much trouble was taken in the Victorian and Edwardian kitchen to set fruit in jelly, the clarity of which was of paramount importance – no cook worth her salt would send up fine fruit set in cloudy jelly. Clarity was achieved by beating egg whites into the syrup to be used, then heating this gently until the egg white coagulated on the surface, drawing up all impurities. At this stage the syrup would be strained through a jelly bag, fruit juice added to flavour, and then the process of clarification repeated if necessary. Isinglass or gelatine would be added and the liquid jelly poured into a mould (rinsed out with cold water in order to make it easier to turn out), and allowed to set; then the fruit would be arranged, set with more jelly, more fruit added and so on. The process, although time consuming, is not difficult. The following recipe, for Raspberry Acid, occurs in *The Cookery Book of Lady Clark of Tillypronie*, and is very useful for jelly making:

Fresh Fruit Jellies

Put 12 lbs of raspberries or strawberries into a pan and pour over them 3 qts. of spring water, to which 5 ozs tartaric acid have been added; let it remain 24 hours, then strain it, taking care not to bruise the fruit; to each pt. of clear liquor add 1½ lbs of loaf sugar finely powdered, stir it frequently, and when the sugar is quite dissolved bottle the syrup, pouring it through a muslin. Cork and seal well down. The whole to be done cold, nothing is boiled.

To make a raspberry or strawberry jelly use 1 pint (500ml) of this fruit syrup: soak ¾ oz (18g) of gelatine in 2 tablespoons (30ml) water, heat the syrup to blood heat, add the gelatine and pour it in a mould to turn out when required.

This charming idea comes from Mrs Beeton's *Book of Household Management*, and makes a very pretty decoration for a Christmas cake. Egg white can be used instead of butter.

To Frost Holly Leaves

Procure some nice sprigs of holly; pick the leaves from the stalks, and wipe them with a clean cloth free from all moisture; then place them on a dish near the fire, to get thoroughly dry, but not too near to shrivel the leaves; dip them into oiled butter, sprinkle over them some coarsely-powdered sugar, and dry them before the fire for about 10 minutes. They should be kept in a dry place, as the least damp would spoil their appearance. These may be made at any time; but are more suitable for winter garnishes, when fresh flowers are not easily obtained.

GRAVY BROWNING

'Browning' is often called for in old recipes, and has nothing to do with packet gravy browning. It is a good basic condiment, and this recipe for it from Mrs Raffald's *The Experienced English Housekeeper* is as good as any. It is very useful to use in recipes such as the Ragoût of Beans on p.36; it adds a good deal to a soup or casserole, and keeps well in the fridge. It is also ideal for adding to vegetarian dishes. It would have been made in considerable quantities in the kitchens of large houses.

1oz (25g) butter
4oz (125g) sugar
1pt (500ml) red wine
½oz (12g) whole allspice
2 blades mace
6 cloves

4 shallots, peeled and
*   finely chopped*
grated rind of 1 lemon
3 tablespoons (45ml)
*   mushroom ketchup*

Put the butter and sugar in a heavy saucepan over a medium heat. Stir well until the sugar has melted, then raise the heat so that the syrup caramelises. Have the red wine ready in another pan, heated to just under boiling point. Wrap your pouring hand in a cloth and slowly pour the wine on to the caramel, stirring with a long-handled spoon as you do so; the mixture splutters alarmingly, hence the precautions. Add the rest of the ingredients and simmer for 15 minutes. Strain the browning into a jug and leave it to cool. Bottle when tepid. The butter in the mixture rises to the top when cold and acts as an airtight seal. Use 4 tablespoons (60ml) of browning to ½ pint (250ml) hot water to make a gravy.

TRUST PROPERTIES
MENTIONED IN THIS BOOK

AVON

Clevedon Court
old mulberry tree
Clevedon
BS21 6QU
Tel. Clevedon
(0272) 872257

Dyrham Park
tea-room in Orangery
Dyrham
Nr Chippenham
SN14 8ER
Tel. Abson
(027582) 2501

CAMBRIDGESHIRE

Peckover House
orangery
North Brink
Wisbech
PE13 1JR
Tel. Wisbech
(0945) 583463

Wimpole Hall
collection walnut trees
Arrington
Royston
Herts
SG8 0BW
Tel. Cambridge
(0223) 207257

CHESHIRE

Little Moreton Hall
knot garden
Congleton
CW12 4SD
Tel. Congleton
(0260) 272018

**Quarry Bank Mill
& Apprentice House**
vegetable garden
Wilmslow
SK9 4LA
Tel. Wilmslow
(0625) 527468

Tatton Park
orangery
Knutsford
WA16 6QN
Tel. Knutsford
(0565) 54822/3

CORNWALL

Cotehele
recipe for lemonade
St Dominick
Nr Saltash
PL12 6TA
Tel. Liskeard
(0579) 50434

Lanhydrock
fine kitchens

Bodmin
PL30 5AD

Tel. Bodmin
(0208) 73320

Trerice
orchard

Nr Newquay
TR8 4PG

Tel. Newquay
(0637) 875404

CUMBRIA

Acorn Bank Garden
herb garden

Temple Sowerby
Nr Penrith
CA10 1SP

Tel. Kirkby Thore
(0930) 61893

Hill Top
kitchen

At Near Sawrey
Ambleside
LA22 0LF

Tel. Hawkshead
(09666) 269

Sizergh Castle
hot wall

Nr Kendal
LA8 8AE

Tel. Sedgwick
(053 95) 60070

DERBYSHIRE

Calke Abbey
kitchen garden

Ticknall
DE7 1LE

Tel. Derby
(0332) 863822

Hardwick Hall
herb garden, orchard

Doe Lea
Chesterfield
S44 5QJ

Tel. Chesterfield
(0246) 850430

DEVON

Buckland Abbey
herb garden

Yelverton
PL20 6EY

Tel. Yelverton
(0822) 853607

Saltram
orangery

Plympton
Plymouth
PL7 3UH

Tel. Plymouth
(0752) 336546

DORSET

Hardy's Cottage
orchard

Higher Bockhampton
Nr Dorchester
DT2 8QJ

Tel. Dorchester
(0305) 62366

GLOUCESTERSHIRE

Westbury Court Garden
wall-fruit

Westbury-on-Severn
GL14 1PD

Tel. Westbury-on-Severn
(045 276) 461

HAMPSHIRE

West Green House
potager

Hartley Wintney
Basingstoke
RG27 8JB

HEREFORD & WORCESTER

Berrington Hall
orchard

Nr Leominster
HR6 0DW

Tel. Leominster
(0568) 5721

KENT

St John's Jerusalem Garden

Sutton-at-Hone
Dartford
DA4 9HQ

Scotney Castle Garden
herb garden

Lamberhurst
Tunbridge Wells
TN3 8JN

Tel. Lamberhurst
(0892) 890651

Sissinghurst Castle Garden
herb garden

Sissinghurst
Nr Cranbrook
TN17 2AB

Tel. Cranbrook
(0580) 712850

LINCOLNSHIRE

Gunby Hall
walled garden

Gunby
Nr Spilsby
PE23 5SS

Woolsthorpe Manor
Newton's apple tree

Woolsthorpe
Colsterworth
Nr Grantham

Tel. Grantham
(0476) 860338

LONDON

Fenton House
kitchen garden

Windmill Hill
Hampstead
NW3 6RT

Tel. 071-435 3471

NORFOLK

Blickling Hall
Apple & Almond Soup

Blickling
Norwich
NR11 6NF

Tel. Aylsham
(0263) 733084

Felbrigg Hall
walled garden

Norwich
NR11 8PR

Tel. West Runton
(026 375) 444

Oxburgh Hall
fruit trees

Oxborough
Nr King's Lynn
PE33 9PS

Tel. Gooderstone
(036 621) 258

NORTHAMPTONSHIRE

Canons Ashby House
orchard

Canons Ashby
Daventry
NN11 6SD

Tel. Blakesley
(0327) 860044

NORTHUMBERLAND

Wallington
conservatory

Cambo
Morpeth
NE61 4AR

Tel. Scots' Gap
(067 074) 283

NOTTINGHAMSHIRE

Clumber Park
conservatory

The Estate Office
Clumber Park
Worksop
S80 3AZ

Tel. Worksop
(0909) 476592

OXFORDSHIRE

Greys Court
walled garden
Rotherfield Greys
Henley-on-Thames
RG9 4PG
Tel. Rotherfield Greys
(049 17) 529

SHROPSHIRE

Attingham Park
quince trees
Shrewsbury
SY4 4TP
Tel. Upton Magna
(074 377) 203

SOMERSET

Barrington Court
kitchen garden
Nr Ilminster
TA19 0NQ
Tel. South Petherton
(0460) 40601/52242

Dunster Castle
lemon trees
Dunster
Nr Minehead
TA24 6SL
Tel. Dunster
(0643) 821314

Lytes Cary Manor
herbs
Charlton Mackrell
Somerton
TA11 7HU

Tintinhull House Garden
kitchen garden
Tintinhull
Nr Yeovil
BA22 9PZ

STAFFORDSHIRE

Moseley Old Hall
fruit trees
Moseley Old Hall Lane
Fordhouses
Wolverhampton
WV10 7HY
Tel. Wolverhampton
(0902) 782808

SURREY

Ham House
cherry trees
Ham
Richmond
TW10 7RS
Tel. 081-940 1950

Oakhurst Cottage
soft fruit
Hambledon
Nr Godalming
Tel. Wormley
(042 879) 4733

Polesden Lacey
Nr Dorking
RH5 6BD
Tel. Bookham
(0372) 58203

SUSSEX (EAST)

Bateman's
pear arch
Burwash
Etchingham
TN19 7DS
Tel. Burwash
(0435) 882302

SUSSEX (WEST)

Petworth House
fruit experiments
Petworth
GU28 0AE
Tel. Petworth
(0798) 42207

Standen
medlar, orchard
East Grinstead
RH19 4NE
Tel. East Grinstead
(0342) 323029

Uppark
use of herbs
South Harting
Petersfield
Hampshire
GU31 5QR
Tel. Harting
(0730) 825317 or 825458

WARWICKSHIRE

Charlecote Park
old mulberry tree
Wellesbourne
Warwick
CV35 9ER

Upton House
kitchen garden
Banbury
Oxfordshire
OX15 6HT
Tel. Edge Hill
(029 587) 266

WEST MIDLANDS

Wightwick Manor
fruit trees
Wightwick Bank
Wolverhampton
WV6 8EE
Tel. Wolverhampton
(0902) 761108

WILTSHIRE

The Courts (Garden)
grapes
Holt
Nr Trowbridge
BA14 6RR
Tel. Trowbridge
(0225) 782340

YORKSHIRE

Beningbrough Hall
grapes, kiwi fruit
Shipton-by-Beningbrough
York
YO6 1DD
Tel. York
(0904) 470666

East Riddlesden Hall
soft fruit, herbs
Bradford Road
Keighley
BD20 5EL
Tel. Keighley
(0535) 607075

Nunnington Hall
orchard
Nunnington
York
YO6 5UY
Tel. Nunnington
(04395) 283

WALES

Erddig
orchard
Nr Wrexham
Clwyd
LL13 0YT
Tel. Wrexham
(0978) 355314

Powis Castle
Welshpool
Powys
SY21 8RF
Tel. Welshpool
(0938) 554336

USEFUL ADDRESSES

Herb, salad and vegetable seeds:

Suffolk Herbs
Sawyers Farm
Little Cornard
Sudbury
Suffolk
CO10 0NY

Dried herbs, spices and pot pourri materials:

Culpeper Ltd
Hadstock Road
Linton
Cambridge
CB1 6NJ

Wide range of fruit trees, especially old varieties of apples:

Scotts Nurseries (Merriott) Ltd
Merriott
Somerset
TA16 5PL

Out-of-print and antiquarian cookery books:

Cooks Books
34 Marine Drive
Rottingdean
Sussex
BN2 7HQ

Out-of-print and antiquarian gardening books:

Mary Bland
Augop
Evenjobb
Nr Presteigne
Powys
Wales

Lloyds of Kew
9 Mortlake Terrace
Kew
Richmond
Surrey
TW9 3DT

BIBLIOGRAPHY

Acton, Eliza. *Modern Cookery*, 1847 edn

Allhusen, Dorothy. *A Book of Scents & Dishes*, 1927

Beeton, Mrs Isabella. *The Book of Household Management*, 1891

Boulestin, X. Marcel. *What Shall We Have Today?*, 1931

Bradley, Richard. *New Improvements of Planting & Gardening*, 1734

Bradley, Richard. *The Country Housewife and Lady's Director*, 1753 edn

Clark, Lady, of Tillypronie. *The Cookery Book of*, 1909

Dods, Mistress Margaret. *The Cook & Housewife's Manual*, c.1885

Evelyn, John. *Acetaria*, 1699

Francatelli, Charles Elme. *The Modern Cook*, 1874 edn

Francatelli, Charles Elme. *The Cook's Guide*, 1875(?)

Gerard, John. *The Herbal*, 1633 edn

Glasse, Hannah. *The Art of Cookery Made Plain and Easy*, 1747 edn

Hill, John. *Eden, or a Compleat Body of Gardening*, 1757

Leyel, Mrs C. F. *The Gentle Art of Cookery*, 1925

Loudon, John Claudius. *The Encyclopaedia of Gardening*, 1822

Markham, Gervase. *The English Housewife*, 1653

Mawe, Thomas & Abercrombie, John. *Every Man his own Gardener*, 1829

Parkinson, John. *A Garden of Pleasant Flowers*, 1629 edn

Raffald, Elizabeth. *The Experienced English Housekeeper*, 1794 edn

Rundell, Mrs. *A New System of Domestic Economy*, 1818 edn

Spry, Constance. *Come into the Garden, Cook*, 1942

Tusser, Thomas. *Five Hundred Points of Good Husbandry*, 1573 (edited by Dorothy Hartley, 1931)

Watts, Elizabeth. *The Orchard and Fruit Garden*, c.1900

INDEX